NEW STUDIES IN BIBLICAL THEOLOGY 1

Series editor: D. A. Carson

Possessed
by
God

A NEW TESTAMENT
THEOLOGY OF
SANCTIFICATION AND
HOLINESS

David Peterson

APOLLOS (an imprint of Inter-Varsity Press),
38 De Montfort Street, Leicester LE1 7GP, England

First published 1995
Reprinted 2000

British Library Cataloguing in Publication Data
A catalogue record for this book is available from the British Library.

ISBN 0–85111–510–1

Set in Baskerville
Photoset by Parker Typesetting Service, Leicester
Printed in Great Britain by Creative Print and Design (Wales), Ebbw Vale

Contents

To the memory of
Gilbert Samuel Peterson
(1919–95)

Series preface

New Studies in Biblical Theology is a series of monographs that address key issues in the discipline of biblical theology. Contributions to the series focus on one or more of three areas: 1. the nature and status of biblical theology, including its relations with other disciplines (*e.g.* historical theology, exegesis, systematic theology, historical criticism, narrative theology); 2. the articulation and exposition of the structure of thought of a particular biblical writer or corpus; and 3. the delineation of a biblical theme across all or part of the biblical corpora.

Above all these monographs are creative attempts to help thinking Christians understand their Bibles better. The series aims simultaneously to instruct and to edify, to interact with the current literature, and to point the way ahead. In God's universe, mind and heart should not be divorced: in this series we will try not to separate what God has joined together. While the end-notes interact with the best of the scholarly literature, the text is uncluttered with untransliterated Greek and Hebrew, and tries to avoid too much technical jargon. The volumes are written within the framework of confessional evangelicalism, but there is always an attempt at thoughtful engagement with the sweep of the relevant literature.

I am delighted that the inaugural volume in the series is by David Peterson, and on a topic of perennial interest to any thoughtful Christian. But Dr Peterson's treatment is far from hackneyed or trivial. His aim is to show that much of the New Testament treatment of sanctification stresses what used to be called 'positional sanctification' or the like – and that much godly living, Christian assurance, stable faith and Christian maturity stem from a firm grasp of what the Bible says in this regard.

D. A. Carson
Trinity Evangelical Divinity School,
Deerfield, Illinois

Preface

The chapters which comprise this book are based upon the Annual Moore College Lectures delivered in Sydney, Australia, in August 1994. I am especially grateful to the principal, Dr Peter Jensen, for the invitation to give five public lectures in this series and for his own careful critique of my work. I am also indebted to students, fellow faculty members and visitors for their questions, challenges and encouragements. Many have helped me to obtain a better view of the Bible's teaching in this critical area and have shown me how to apply it to the contemporary scene. Professor D. A. Carson and Dr Peter O'Brien offered many valuable suggestions for revision as the lectures were being prepared for publication. Special thanks are also due to Mr Tony Payne, who prepared the illustrations that show the link between related biblical themes at various stages in the argument. I dedicate this book to the memory of my father, who went to be with his Lord on 6 February 1995.

Abbreviations

AV	Authorized Bible.
ET	English translation.
LXX	Septuagint (Greek Version of the Old Testament).
NASB	New American Standard Bible.
NEB	New English Bible.
NIV	New International Version.
NRSV	New Revised Standard Version.
RSV	Revised Standard Version.
TDNT	*Theological Dictionary of the New Testament,* ed. G. Kittel & G. Friedrich, trans. and ed. G. W. Bromiley, 10 vols., Grand Rapids: Eerdmans, 1964–76.

Introduction

Holiness: a neglected priority?

Considering the passion for holiness expressed by writers and preachers in former generations, James Packer may be right to claim that 'holiness is a neglected priority throughout the modern church generally' and 'specifically a fading glory in today's evangelical world' (1984: 99). Very little attention is given to the subject in academic circles. Popular studies appear from time to time, but these often lack biblical insight and theological depth. Serious teaching about the theme is rarely heard in our churches. Meanwhile, much of our contemporary church life seems superficial, self-indulgent and compromised. All too often, we are greeted with media reports about the scandalous behaviour of prominent Christians or about the hypocrisy of this group or that.

Packer considers that a preoccupation with other issues has kept us from a zealous pursuit of holiness. Yet his illustrations beg the question about what really constitutes holiness in the New Testament. For example, he implies that defending the biblical faith from diminution and distortion and struggling to mobilize outreach in mission and evangelism are alternatives to the pursuit of holiness. This suggests that holiness is essentially a matter of moral purity. Scripture, on the other hand, indicates that it involves standing against secularism and idolatry in all its forms, so that defending and propagating the faith are important dimensions to the sanctified life.

Much more significantly, in my opinion, Packer argues:

> Evangelicals today are disillusioned with what has long been put to them as 'holiness teaching' (higher life, deeper life, victorious life, Keswick, entire

sanctification, or any other version of the 'second-blessing' theme). What they have heard now strikes them as sterile, superficial, stunting real growth and irrelevant to today's perplexities and conflicts about Christian living (1984: 100).

What we need is an approach that is faithful to Scripture, applicable to our contemporary situation, instructed by history's debates, yet advancing beyond the inadequacies of previous formulations. Despite the significant work of Packer and others, there is room for a fresh look at the subject, with a particular focus on what the New Testament teaches about the way holiness is achieved and expressed.

Conflicting theologies of sanctification and holiness

Two recent volumes highlight different perspectives that have been adopted by Christians over the centuries. One deals with the Wesleyan, Reformed, Pentecostal, Keswick and Augustinian–Dispensational approaches (see Dieter *et al* 1987), the other with the Lutheran, Reformed, Wesleyan, Pentecostal and Contemplative views (see Alexander 1988).[1] Each position is critiqued by contributors from other traditions. A fruitful dialogue is set up, in which points of agreement and disagreement are made clear. Such books provide an excellent introduction to the subject, but lead me to conclude that, if any advance is to be made, there is more work to be done at the level of biblical interpretation.

Forty years ago, Christians in my part of the world were heavily involved in debates about this subject. Some emerged from that period angry and hurt. Many wanted to abandon the terminology altogether, preferring to speak about the justified life, repentance, faith, righteousness and godliness. Much is lost, however, by refusing to use the language of sanctification and holiness in a biblical way. Indeed, a major failing of many expositions of this subject has been the lack of a thorough and systematic investigation of the relevant terms and their use in Scripture.

The Bible has also been used selectively in much of the literature on this subject. For example, the teaching of Hebrews on sanctification is often ignored, though the writer's exhortation to pursue the holiness 'without which no-one will see the Lord' (Heb. 12:14) is given great prominence. Without explanation or reason, certain texts in the letters of Paul are also given much greater attention than others. The assumption is generally made that sanctification is simply the process by which we become more and more holy.

In systematic theology, sanctification has become the basket into which every theme related to Christian life and growth has been placed. Anthony Hoekema typically defines it as:

> . . . that gracious operation of the Holy Spirit, involving our responsible participation, by which he delivers us from the pollution of sin, renews our entire nature according to the image of God, and enables us to live lives that are pleasing to him (1989: 192).[2]

For reasons that I shall outline in the following chapters, this is an inadequate definition. It obscures the distinctive meaning and value of the terminology in the New Testament, confusing sanctification with renewal and transformation. Theologians are clearly bound to show how the doctrines of regeneration and renewal, justification and sanctification, spiritual growth and glorification, relate to one another. But this can only be done in a satisfactory way when the particular contribution of each theme is isolated and understood in its biblical dimensions.

The foundational importance of definitive sanctification

Although it is unclear from his definition, Hoekema rightly notes the *definitive* aspect to sanctification in the New Testament (1989: 202–209).[3] Several texts point to the fact that God sanctifies his people once and for all, through the work of Christ on the cross. Other texts link sanctification with conversion or baptism into Christ, highlighting the work of the Holy Spirit through the gospel, consecrating believers to God as his holy people under the New Covenant. Yet Hoekema does not give this teaching the weight that it deserves. There is an assumption that sanctification is mainly viewed in *progressive* terms in the

New Testament. Little is made of definitive sanctification as a basis and motivation for holy living.

Klaus Bockmuehl more helpfully begins his exposition of the subject by defining sanctification in the Old Testament as 'the act or process by which people or things are cleansed and dedicated to God, ritually and morally' (1988: 613). Turning to the New Testament, he observes that cleansing and dedication continue to be dominant notes when the terminology of sanctification and holiness is used. Sanctification is a state in which believers find themselves because of the work of Christ and the operation of his Spirit in their lives. They are called to remain in that state 'by living in correspondence to their given holiness' (614).[4] It is also a state to which they must strive, which they must 'pursue', or 'complete'. In sum, sanctification in the New Testament is seen as 'a one-time event and as a process, the believers *being* and *becoming* holy and *acting* correspondingly' (614).[5]

This is a much more helpful approach to the evidence and one which I want to explore and develop. I will argue that definitive sanctification is a more important theme in the New Testament than has generally been acknowledged. Rightly understood, this doctrine is a key to holy living and a way through the impasse created by much previous debate. God calls us and enables us in Christ to live as those possessed by God and empowered by his Holy Spirit. This is the theme of the first three chapters of this book. The fourth chapter then examines New Testament exhortations to pursue holiness and considers the sense in which sanctification is a process of 'becoming' and 'acting'. Much debate about sanctification has focused on the interpretation of Romans 6 – 8. Consequently, chapter five provides an overview of that section, in the light of Paul's teaching about sanctification elsewhere. Biblical promises of transformation and growth are then considered, as the concluding chapter attempts to integrate other strands of teaching about the Christian life with what I have discovered about sanctification.

Chapter One

The biblical starting-point

Christians at the end of the twentieth century may be surprised to discover how controversial the doctrine of sanctification has been throughout history. Vigorous debates have taken place about the nature of holiness and how it is acquired.[1] In some quarters, sanctification has been almost exclusively understood in ritual terms. In others, it has been associated with asceticism and various forms of self-discipline. More commonly, however, it has been explained as *a process of moral and spiritual transformation,* flowing from justification by faith.

From the moment of initiation into Christ, growth in holiness has been expected in the context of everyday life and experience. Change has been viewed as the work of the Holy Spirit, but with varying degrees of emphasis on human effort and the need to follow humanly-devised programmes for transformation. Progress has sometimes been sought by withdrawal from the world, to encounter God through individual spiritual exercises.

Some Christian traditions have highlighted the need for a *crisis experience* for sanctification. This has been sought as the gift of God in answer to faith, as a 'second blessing' beyond conversion. Various 'higher-life' movements have combined such teaching with different degrees of perfectionism. Adherents have been encouraged to expect miraculous character transformation or a new level of spirituality, making possible significant progress in holiness.

Theology and biblical interpretation

Why do Christians differ so much on a topic like this? Fundamentally because of the way we interpret Scripture. A primary task for theologians is to survey the Bible's teaching on a given subject and to show how the evidence can be meaningfully arranged and expressed. An associated task is to show

how the doctrine that is formulated relates to other biblical themes. Much confusion about sanctification has arisen because these theological activities have been pursued in ways that are methodologically unsound.

In the first place, inadequate attention has been paid to the use of holiness terminology in the New Testament and to passages which deal specifically with the subject of sanctification. Presuppositions about its nature and purpose seem to have determined the selection and interpretation of key texts. Writers have often been preoccupied with establishing the place of sanctification within the framework of a given theological system rather than letting the biblical evidence speak for itself. For many, sanctification has become such a broad concept that its particular New Testament meaning has been obscured. Most importantly, the background of Old Testament theology, which regularly shapes the writings of the New Testament, has not been sufficiently taken into account.

With such problems in mind, my plan is firstly to explore the theological roots of New Testament thinking in a broad survey of Old Testament principles and practices. I will then examine the way New Testament writers adapt the concepts of sanctification and holiness that were part of their biblical inheritance. From time to time, critical passages will be approached in the light of later doctrinal questions and debates. Related passages and themes will then be discussed in connection with the teaching of those key passages. The overall aim will be to hear afresh God's challenge to holiness, encouraged by the promises on which it is grounded and guided by the teaching with which it is associated.

The holiness of God

First and foremost, holiness in Scripture is a description of God and his character. God is regularly identified as 'the Holy One' (*e.g.* Jb. 6:10; Is. 40:25; 43:15; Ezk. 39:7; Ho. 11:9; Hab. 1:12; 3:3) or 'the Holy One of Israel' (*e.g.* 2 Ki. 19:22; Is. 1:4; 43:3; Je. 50:29; 51:5). Isaiah describes him more completely as 'the high and lofty one who inhabits eternity, whose name is Holy' (Is. 57:15). Yet the same prophet goes on to indicate that the Lord who dwells in 'the high and holy place' dwells also with 'those who are contrite and humble in spirit'.

16

A synonym for deity

So essential is holiness to God's character that when Amos speaks of him swearing 'by his holiness' (Am. 4:2), it is the same as saying 'the Lord God has sworn by himself' (Am. 6:8). God's 'arm', God's word and God's spirit are all holy because they belong to him (*e.g.* Is. 52:10; Ps. 105:42; Is. 63:10). Since God's name is so closely associated with his character and person, there is much in the Old Testament about not profaning his holy name (*e.g.* Ex. 20:7; Lv. 20:3; Ezk. 20:39; 36:20; Am. 2:7). Rather, Israel is to trust in his name, to glory in it and to bless it (*e.g.* Ps. 33:21; 1 Ch. 16:10; Ps. 103:1).

The root meaning of the Hebrew noun 'holiness' (*qōḏeš*) and the adjective 'holy' (*qāḏôš*) is separation.[2] The Greek Bible uses *hagios* and some of its derivatives as the equivalent of the Hebrew. This terminology refers to the distinctness or otherness of God's character, activities and words. God's holiness is particularly associated with his majesty, sovereignty and awesome power (*e.g.* Ex. 15:11–12; 19:10–25; Is. 6:1–4). As the one who is supreme over all, he is transcendent, exalted and different from everything he has made. He cannot be compared with the gods of human imagination or be judged by human standards.

> God is separate and distinct because he is God. He is not separated from this, that, or the other because of any of his attributes or qualities or the like (Snaith 1944: 30).[3]

God alone is holy in himself.

An important dimension to God's separateness and distinctness is his *moral purity and perfection*. He is presented in the Old Testament as ethically unique, 'too pure to behold evil' and unable to tolerate wrong (Hab. 1:12–13; *cf.* Is. 1:4–20; 35:8). He must act with holy justice when his people rebel against him, yet his love will not allow him to wipe them out. Speaking through Hosea, he explains his restoration of them in these terms, 'for I am God and no mortal, the Holy One in your midst, and I will not come in wrath' (Ho. 11:9). This means that his love is also 'holy'. God loves with an incomparable and distinctive love.

17

The holiness of God revealed

From the time of the exodus from Egypt, the Lord was recognized by Israel as being 'majestic in holiness, awesome in splendour, doing wonders' (Ex. 15:11).[4] The defeat of Pharaoh and his gods and the passage of Israel through the sea revealed the uniqueness of the God who had always been there, sustaining his creation, making promises to the patriarchs and fulfilling his plans. 'The Song of Moses' declares that the Lord, though different from the gods of human imagination, and finally beyond description, had been met in history – in his saving acts and in the revelation of his glory associated with those wonderful deeds.

There were two sides to God's holiness which Israel witnessed in the exodus and subsequently. He brought *judgment* upon those who flouted his purposes and *salvation* to those who trusted in him. At Mount Sinai, the revelation of his holiness made him seem threatening and unapproachable (Ex. 19:10–25; *cf.* Jos. 24:19; 1 Sa. 6:20). But the giving of the law was an expression of his mercy and grace and a sign of his intention to dwell among his people as 'the Holy One' (*cf.* Ex. 29:42–46; Ho. 11:9; Is. 57:15). The tabernacle in the wilderness and the temple in Jerusalem were to be the physical means of identifying and responding to his kingly presence in their midst.

At a later stage in Israel's history, the prophet Isaiah had a vision of the holiness of God encapsulating much of what had been revealed before. The Lord appeared to him in the Jerusalem temple as king of the universe, enthroned in a heavenly palace (Is. 6:1–4), with his supernatural attendants proclaiming: 'Holy, holy, holy is the LORD of hosts; the whole earth is full of his glory'.[5] Even though the holiness of God cannot be adequately conveyed in vision or word, angelic beings declared that it could be encountered in our universe, which is like a vast temple dedicated to his use and the display of his glory. God's glory is his holiness revealed.

Overcome and exposed by what he experienced, the prophet confessed that there was no hope for him or for rebellious Israel in the presence of such a God. 'Woe is me! I am lost,' he said, 'for I am a man of unclean lips, and I live among a people of unclean lips; yet my eyes have seen the King, the LORD of hosts!' (Is. 6:5). As the representative of God's people, Isaiah acknowledged their rejection of God's rule and their failure to worship him appropriately. Judgment on their sin would inevitably follow. With a burning coal from the altar of incense, however, a seraph expressed God's extraordinary mercy: 'Now that this has touched your lips, your guilt has departed and your sin is blotted out' (6:6–7). The paradox of holiness is that God acts to judge everything that is unholy and yet provides a way of cleansing and sanctification for sinners.

Purified from sin, the prophet was able to stand in God's presence and be commissioned as his mouthpiece. His task was to announce God's judgment on that unrepentant nation until all was fulfilled (6:8–13). Yet, even beyond terrible devastation and destruction, God's purpose for his people would continue. The cleansing and preservation of the prophet himself anticipated the salvation of a remnant, identified here as 'the holy seed' (6:13; see Motyer 1993: 80).[6] God's 'offspring' would be holy because of his actions on their behalf. Purified and preserved by the Holy One, the inhabitants of a renewed Jerusalem would become a symbol of hope for the whole creation (*cf.* 4:2–6; 65:17–25).

The holiness of God's people

As the Holy One, God cannot be associated with anything that is 'unholy'. Nevertheless, many Old Testament passages indicate that holiness can be attributed or imparted to people or objects because they are cleansed and consecrated to the Lord and his service. The use of the Hebrew verb *qādaš* is especially interesting in this connection. It is variously translated 'to set apart, consecrate, hallow, sanctify, treat as holy'. In the Greek Bible it is rendered by the verb *hagiazein*. The cultic or ritual dimension of sanctification is foundational, but behind this lies an even more fundamental notion of sanctification by divine election and redemption.

Sanctified by God's initiative

For Israel, holiness was to be found in a relationship with the Holy One. The Lord himself sanctified Israel, by rescuing his people from Egypt, bringing them to himself at Mount Sinai, and giving them his law (Ex. 19:1–6; 20:1–6; *cf.* Ex. 31:13). A common factor in the three terms describing Israel's vocation in

Exodus 19:5–6 ('my treasured possession', 'a priestly kingdom', 'a holy nation') is the note of *separation* from the nations, so as to be uniquely at God's disposal. They were to demonstrate what it means to live under the direct rule of God, which is actually 'the biblical aim for the whole world' (Dumbrell 1984: 87).[7] As such, they were to be the means by which God's original promise to Abraham of bringing blessing to all the nations would be enacted (*cf.* Gn. 12:1–3). As a priestly kingdom, they were to serve the Lord exclusively and thus be a people through whom his character and will might be displayed to the world.[8]

When they came to Sinai, Moses was told to consecrate them ritually, to prepare for a unique encounter with God (Ex. 19:14). They were already a holy nation because God had drawn them to himself, but now they would discover the awesome implications of being in a special relationship with him. Even the priests were required to 'consecrate themselves', lest he 'break out against them' (19:22). The point of these instructions was to teach Israel about God's overpowering holiness. Even 'a holy people' could only approach him and relate to him on the terms that he laid down. A system of mediation was necessary to prevent the Israelites from being destroyed by God's holiness (19:22, 24).[9]

Sanctification as a way of life

After Sinai, the ritual provisions of the covenant were meant to sustain Israel as a holy nation. Elaborate instructions were given for consecrating Aaron and his sons as priests (Ex. 28:3, 41; 29:1, 21, 27; *cf.* Lv. 8). Here the emphasis was on separation, purification and initiation into a distinctive role before God, as representatives of the people. Levites were also set apart 'to do service' for Israel and assist the priests (Nu. 8:14–19). Both groups were consecrated to God so that Israel could remain a consecrated people and continue to draw near to God in his holiness.

The altar was to be consecrated by an atoning sacrifice and by anointing, so that the altar became 'most holy' (Ex. 29:36–37).[10] Similarly the tent of meeting, the ark of the covenant, and the furniture and utensils of the sanctuary were to be consecrated by anointing with 'a holy anointing oil' (Ex. 30:26–30). Holiness demanded separation with respect to places, times, persons and acts. In different ways, the demand for separation from the beliefs and practices of the surrounding nations was to impinge on the life of every Israelite.

The tabernacle, and later the temple, would constantly represent God's holy presence in the midst of his people and his rule over them. The covenant relationship established by God contained at its heart the assurance that he would be their God and they would be his people (*e.g.* Gn. 17:7–8; Ex. 6:7). Consequently, he would be uniquely with them, to fulfil his purposes and bring blessing to them (*e.g.* Gn. 28:13–15; Ex. 3:7–8).[11] God's sanctifying presence would continue to mark them as a holy people and demand holiness of living as a response.

Since the Holy One had brought the Israelites into a special relationship with himself by redeeming them and dwelling amongst them, the fundamental demand of the levitical code was 'You shall be holy, for I am holy' (Lv. 11:44–45; 19:2; 20:7, 26). In this framework of thought, the command to 'sanctify yourselves' (11:44, Heb. *hitqaddistem*, Gk. *hagiasthēsesthe*) meant 'live as those who know God's character and will and delight to please him'. By keeping his ritual, moral and social laws, the people of Israel would not profane his holy name before the nations. Rather, they would demonstrate God's virtues and the benefit of being 'a people holy to the LORD . . . chosen out of all the peoples on earth to be his people, his treasured possession' (Dt. 14:2).[12]

Pollution and sin were to be avoided in every aspect of life, and there was to be a complete break with every form of idolatry and false religion. Separation from the nations and consecration to God were two different facets of their exclusive relationship with the Lord. When transgression occurred, rites of purification were available for the restoration of 'cleanness' and holiness (Wenham 1979: 20).[13] The Lord who had sanctified them, by bringing them out of Egypt to be their God, would thus be sanctified or treated as holy among his people by their beliefs and practices (*cf.* Lv. 22:31–33; Nu. 15:40–41; Is. 8:13).

Throughout the Old Testament, different emphases or ideals of holiness may be observed.

> For the prophets it was a cleanness of social justice, for the priests a cleanness of proper ritual and main-tenance of separation, for the sages it was a cleanness

of inner integrity and individual moral acts (Gammie
1989: 196).

Nevertheless, there is a shifting and blending of these ideals
in various parts of the canon, so that it is possible to see a
unified demand for purity before God. This is expressed in
different ways, according to the context. But the common
element is an awareness of God's initiative in making himself
known as the Holy One, taking possession of Israel as his own,
and requiring his people to live in the light of his self-
revelation in their midst.

Sanctifying the Lord

Sabbath-keeping was to be a particularly important mark of
Israel as a holy nation. God's people were to sanctify or hallow
the seventh day by using it in the way that he decreed. Ordinary
work would cease so that the day could be set aside to express
the special relationship between Israel and the God who created
the universe (*cf.* Ex. 31:12–17; Ezk. 20:12). Keeping the sabbath
as a holy day was to be Israel's way of honouring the Holy One
and acknowledging that he was the one who sanctified them
(Ex. 31:13). Here the sanctifying work of God refers to the
whole process of bringing the Israelites into an exclusive
relationship with himself by rescuing them from slavery and
establishing them as a holy people under the rule of his word. As
a sanctified people, they would be able to sanctify the Lord by
sanctifying the sabbath!

On one critical occasion, Moses and Aaron failed to sanctify
the Lord or maintain his holiness before the Israelites (Nu.
20:12, Heb. *lᵉhaqdîšēnî*, Gk. *hagiasai me*). They did not trust him
and carry out his instructions before the people exactly as they
were told. Their rebellion was so serious that they were
prevented from leading the people into the promised land
(Nu. 20:12, 24). God's judgment on Moses and Aaron, together
with his merciful provision of water for the quarrelsome
Israelites, are probably both included in the statement that the
Lord 'showed his holiness' (20:13, Heb. *wayyiqqādēš*, Gk.
hēgiasthē en autois) at Meribah. This incident, which is mentioned again in several contexts (Nu. 27:14; Dt. 32:51; Ps.
106:32–33), indicates that God acts to sanctify himself before

his people, when they refuse to acknowledge his holiness appropriately (*cf.* Lv. 10:1–3).

This latter point emerges most powerfully in Ezekiel's prophecy about the return of the exiled Israelites from Babylon to Jerusalem. God promised to sanctify himself or manifest his holiness among them in the sight of the nations, by rescuing them and restoring them (Ezk. 20:41; 28:22, 25). God had to sanctify his great name in this way because it had been profaned among the nations by his people and he wished the nations to know that he is the Lord (36:23).[14] Ezekiel goes on to indicate that this revelation of God's holiness will involve the restoration of his covenant with Israel, the re-establishment of Davidic kingship and the setting up of his sanctuary or dwelling-place among them for evermore (37:24–28).

In Ezekiel's teaching there are once again indications that it is the Lord who sanctifies Israel (Ezk. 36:28; *cf.* Sir. 33:12; Jud. 6:19). He did this at the return from exile as he did it in the exodus from Egypt. He brought his people to know him and trust him again by a great act of redemption, restoring them to the promised land and dwelling amongst them in a distinctive way to bless them. In doing this, his ultimate concern was to sanctify himself or *manifest his holiness in Israel for the blessing of the nations.*[15]

Conclusion

Since God is the Holy One, incomparable in majesty, splendour and purity, he is the only source of true holiness for his people. He sanctifies his own name, displaying his holiness by acting in judgment and salvation and calling upon them to acknowledge him as the Holy One. Holiness cannot simply be acquired by human effort. It is a status or condition which God imparts to those whom he chooses to bring into a special relationship with himself through covenant and redemption. But it is a status that carries with it particular responsibilities.

Various rituals are prescribed in the Old Testament to enable Israel to express her consecrated status and remain in that distinct relationship with the Holy One. Yet the ritual and the moral requirements of the law are closely linked, so that God's holiness is acknowledged by faithfulness to his demands in every sphere of life. God appeals to his people 'to remain conscious of the sanctity with which he has sanctified them, and to walk and live accordingly' (Berkouwer 1952: 23).[16] With regard to God himself, holiness implies transcendence, uniqueness and purity. With regard to God's people, holiness means *being set apart for a relationship with the Holy One, to display his character in every sphere of life.*

Separation was to be expressed in time and space and ritual. Sanctification was primarily a technical term of the cult, connoting both cleansing and consecration. It was also to be demonstrated in the moral and social sphere and in breaking with every form of idolatry and false religion. In the final analysis, Israel's task as a 'holy nation' was to sanctify the Lord before the nations by responding appropriately to him as the Holy One. God's honour and the salvation of the nations were at stake here. As Israel pursued the path of holiness, God promised to bless her and make her a blessing to the nations.

Approaching the New Testament

I want to show how such biblical–theological perspectives are adopted and adapted by the writers of the New Testament. By way of introduction, I will make four claims which I hope to substantiate as this book progresses.

1. Just as Israel was made holy by God's saving activity in the time of Moses, and again in the restoration after the Babylonian Exile, so sanctification in the New Testament is an integral part of the redemptive work of Jesus Christ. It is regularly portrayed as a once-for-all, definitive act and primarily has to do with the holy status or position of those who are 'in Christ'.

2. Just as Israel was maintained as a holy people by God's presence in their midst and his provision of the priesthood and rituals of the Mosaic Covenant, so Christians are sustained in holiness by the ongoing presence of the Holy Spirit and the trust that he gives in the finished work of Christ. The essential work of the Spirit is to enable belief in the gospel, so that the blessings it offers may be continually enjoyed by God's people.

3. Just as there were lifestyle implications for those who knew the Holy One of Israel and were convinced that they belonged to him in an exclusive way, so Christians are called to live out the practical consequences of knowing God in Jesus Christ and of being consecrated by his saving work. Everything that is said about moral change and personal transformation in the New

Testament is to be related to God's sanctifying initiative in Christ.

4. Just as sanctification in the Old Testament meant being separated from the beliefs and practices of the nations, to be devoted to God and the doing of his will, so sanctification in Christ has to do with a profound re-orientation of values and behaviour. Beginning with the 'heart' and reaching out to touch the life and witness of God's people at every level, God's word and God's Spirit bring change and transformation. In us and through us, something of God's holiness is revealed to the world.

Chapter Two

Sanctified in Christ

Sanctification is commonly regarded as a process of moral and spiritual transformation following conversion. In the New Testament, however, it primarily refers to God's way of taking possession of us in Christ, setting us apart to belong to him and to fulfil his purpose for us. Sanctification certainly has present and ongoing effects, but when the verb 'to sanctify' (Gk. *hagiazein*) and the noun 'sanctification' (Gk. *hagiasmos*) are used, the emphasis is regularly on the saving work of God in Christ, applied to believers through the ministry of the Holy Spirit.

Language used of Israel's status and calling as the people of God in the Old Testament is employed to describe the distinctive role and function of Christians in the world. Ritual consecration to God, which is such a prominent feature of the Mosaic law, is replaced by the consecrating work of Jesus in his death and resurrection. Believers are definitively consecrated to God in order to live dedicated and holy lives, to his glory.

The teaching of Jesus: sanctified by the sanctifying of the Son of God

Jesus offers very little direct teaching on the theme of holiness and sanctification. He speaks as a Jew of his time when he refers to the sanctuary in Jerusalem as 'the holy place' (Mt. 24:15) and observes that a gift is 'sanctified' by being placed upon the temple altar (Mt. 23:19; *cf.* 23:17). Enigmatically he warns, 'Do not give what is holy to dogs; and do not throw your pearls before swine' (Mt. 7:6). More profoundly he echoes the sentiment of many Old Testament passages when he teaches his disciples to pray for God's name to be 'hallowed' (Mt. 6:9; *cf.* Lk. 11:2).

At the same time, Jesus implies that Old Testament prescriptions about defilement and purification are about to be transcended (Mt. 15:1–20; *cf.* Mk. 7:1–23).[1] In the Sermon on the Mount, he identifies his disciples as the true Israel (Mt. 5:1–16) and speaks about the need for them to manifest a righteousness exceeding that of the scribes and Pharisees (5:17–48).[2] In various ways throughout the Gospels, he refers to the gift of the Holy Spirit as the means by which disciples will be sustained in a new and distinct relationship with the Father (*e.g.* Mt. 12:28; 28:19–20; Mk. 13:11; Lk. 11:13; 12:12; 24:49; Jn. 3:5–8; 14:26; 20:22).

Most importantly, in the Gospel of John, Jesus uses the language of sanctification with reference to his own role as the saviour and sanctifier of others (Jn. 10:36; 17:19). A comprehensive picture of the sanctification he makes available is then set out in the prayer of John 17. Delivered in the presence of his Jewish disciples, this prayer promises a sanctification fulfilling and surpassing the sanctification experienced by Israel under the Law. These Johannine references are a fitting place to begin a survey of New Testament thinking on this subject.[3]

The sanctification of the Son of God

According to John 10:36, Jesus took the initiative in describing himself as 'the one whom the Father has sanctified and sent into the world'. Significantly, he said this during the annual Feast of Dedication, which commemorated the reconsecration of the temple altar, after it had been defiled by pagan invaders. Jesus' language implies that he was 'set apart' as the pre-incarnate Son for a mission that would fulfil and surpass the ministry of altar and temple in Israel (*cf.* Jn. 2:19–22).

As noted in the previous chapter, altar, priests and sanctuary were consecrated in Old Testament times, to enable God's people to relate to him appropriately. Prophets were also consecrated by God to communicate his truth to them (Je. 1:5; *cf.* Sir. 45:1–5). In John's perspective, Jesus fulfils these functions by being the Word become flesh (Jn. 1:14) and the good shepherd who lays down his life for God's sheep (Jn. 10:11–30).

Aware that the Father had sanctified and sent him for a specific purpose, Jesus was determined to devote himself exclusively to the Father and the doing of his will (*cf.* Jn. 4:34; 6:38). In the so-called high-priestly prayer of John 17 he says, 'for their sakes I sanctify myself, so that they may also be sanctified in truth' (17:19). The Fourth Gospel makes it plain that the ultimate purpose of the Son's mission is his death, resurrection and return to glory (*e.g.* 1:29; 10:17–18; 11:49–52; 18:11; 19:30). When he claims to sanctify or set himself aside 'for their sakes' (Gk. *hyper autōn*), the language is evocative of atonement passages elsewhere in the New Testament (*e.g.* Mk. 14:24; Lk. 22:19; Jn. 6:51; 1 Cor. 11:24). Jesus dedicates himself to become *a sacrifice for sins*.[4] His teaching about the sanctification of believers is presented in this significant context.

As 'the Lamb of God who takes away the sin of the world' (Jn. 1:29, 36) and as 'the good shepherd', who 'lays down his life for the sheep' (10:11, 17–18), the Messiah must die to deliver Israel from God's judgment and to make it possible for believers to be drawn together to God from every nation (11:49–53; 12:20–33). Disciples are separated from the world and from the evil one (17:15–16), by being consecrated in the truth of God's word (17:17). By this means they are liberated to bring blessing to the world as the agents of Christ (17:18).

The sanctification of disciples

Jesus' first request for his disciples in the prayer of John 17 is expressed in these terms: 'Holy Father, protect them in your name that you have given me, so that they may be one, as we are one' (17:11). As in Old Testament teaching, God is regarded as holy and those who belong to him must share his holiness. So Jesus prays that they may be kept 'in' or 'by' the power of God's name (Gk. *en tō onomati sou*), which is a way of speaking about God's *character*, supremely revealed in the person of his Son, the Word-made-flesh (1:14–18), and in the word or teaching that he delivered to his followers (17:14).

When Jesus was there in person, showing them the Father, he was able to protect them in that name from perishing (17:12). All were kept from apostasy except Judas, 'the one destined to be lost'. Jesus expects that his approaching death and return to the Father will expose them afresh to danger from 'the world' and 'the evil one' (17:14–15).[5] Putting it negatively, he wants his followers to be delivered from the control of Satan and every force of evil in the world.

Although disciples are chosen 'out of the world' (15:19), Jesus does not want them to be disengaged or removed from the world (17:15). Rather, they are to be *kept as a unity* (17:11), even as the Father and the Son are one, knowing that they *do not belong to the world* (17:14, 16), as Jesus does not belong to the world. In the Old

Testament, Israel's sanctification was linked with the call to be distinct from the beliefs and practices of the nations. Jesus' prayer for his followers is that they might similarly be kept from being overwhelmed by the world and its values, so that they might be devoted or 'sanctified' to the Father and his values (17:17–19).

The goal of separation from the world, and from Satan as its ruler, is that disciples might actually be *sent into the world*, just as the Son was 'sanctified' and sent by the Father (10:36), to bring the blessing of eternal life to the world (17:18). Jesus' prayer anticipates the later commissioning of the apostles for mission (20:21). In other words, it has a special application to the original core group of disciples. Yet he goes on to pray for those who would believe as a result of their testimony (17:20–24). His desire is that we too might share in the unity of the Father and the Son, so that the world might believe he was sent by the Father (17:21), and know that he is the ultimate expression of the Father's love for us (17:23; *cf.* 3:16). Mission is clearly the goal of sanctification in John 17.

Kept in the truth, by word and Spirit

Jesus' prayer for his disciples to be sanctified 'in the truth' (17:17), is really another way of saying 'protect them in your name that you have given me' (17:11) or 'keep them in the truth that I have given them'. The tense of the verb in the expression 'sanctify them' (Gk. *hagiason autous*) does not pinpoint a specific moment in time. A complete and undifferentiated process is usually signified by the Greek aorist in the New Testament.[6] 'Consecrate them to yourself and keep them in that relationship' will be the sense in this context. As already noted, the sanctification of the disciples is closely linked with Jesus' sending of them into the world (17:18).

Even more decisive for an understanding of Jesus' prayer in John 17:17 is his statement in 17:19 ('for their sakes I sanctify myself, so that they also may be sanctified in truth'). Disciples cannot be sanctified and sent into the world until the Son of God consecrates himself to die on their behalf. The purpose of his self-consecration in death is that disciples might be, literally, 'having been sanctified' (Gk. *hēgiasmenoi*). Jesus does not speak of a *crisis* (17:17) and then a *process* (17:19).[7] The Greek perfect passive in 17:19 points rather to a *state* of holiness resulting from his prayer and his saving action on their behalf.

Sanctification 'in the truth' is mentioned in 17:17 and 17:19. The Greek expression *en (tē) alētheia* could be understood instrumentally: the Father will sanctify the followers of Jesus by means of the truth (NIV, 'sanctify them *by* the truth'). But it is also possible that truth is the realm into which they are sanctified (NRSV, 'sanctify them *in* the truth').[8] In the light of Jesus' previous teaching in the Fourth Gospel, this is a significant statement.

The truth which Jesus imparts has the power to set people free from slavery to sin, to serve the living God (Jn. 8:31–36). As we shall see, this is an important aspect of the teaching about sanctification elsewhere in the New Testament. Although it is common to hear the remark that 'mere words' can change nothing, according to Christ's own claim, the words that he speaks are 'spirit and life' (6:63).

Jesus himself is 'the truth', according to John 14:6, but the truth which sanctifies in 17:17 is more specifically the word of God which he gave to the disciples in his teaching (17:14). Believing this, they have already been set apart from the world and the world has hated them for it.[9] Jesus indicates that they will be kept as God's holy people by this same word. In practical terms:

> No-one can be 'sanctified' or set apart for the Lord's use without learning to think God's thoughts after him, without learning to live in conformity with the 'word' he has graciously given. By contrast, the heart of 'worldliness', of what makes the world the world (1:9), is fundamental suppression or denial of the truth, profound rejection of God's gracious 'word', his self-disclosure in Christ (Carson 1991: 566).

Surprisingly enough, the Holy Spirit is not mentioned in John 17. But, given the context of Jesus' upper-room discourse in chapters 14–16, the Spirit's work may be implied in Jesus' prayer for their consecration in the truth of God's word.[10] Previously identified as 'the Spirit of truth' (14:17; 15:26; 16:13), the Spirit will remind the apostolic group of everything Jesus said (14:26), testifying on behalf of the Son as they themselves give testimony to Jesus (15:26–27). He will use their witness to prove the world wrong about sin and righteousness and judgment (16:8–11). He will guide them 'into all the truth' and glorify Christ by declaring 'the things that are to come' (16:13–15). So the Spirit authenticates and empowers the witness of the apostles and makes their word the means by which others are drawn into the fellowship of the Father and the Son (17:20–24). We might say that the Spirit works through the apostolic word to sanctify or consecrate a people to God 'in the truth'.

Kept in love

Sanctification in John 17:17 refers to the holy status of those whom Jesus brings to God. It involves a separation from the world and a consecration to the Father that the Son makes possible by his teaching, his prayer, his self-consecration in death, and his sending of the Holy Spirit (16:7). But it is evident from John 17 'that a purely positional standing in Christ or otherworldly experience of him could never effect the witness in the world that Christ prayed for' (Dieter 1987: 32). His desire is for his followers to be brought into such a unity of love with the Father and the Son that the world might believe. If holiness means sharing in the character and life of God, some concrete evidence of this in terms of the loving commitment of disciples to one another is clearly expected.

Love is a vital expression of the sanctification for which Jesus prays. But there is no suggestion in this context that love is perfected through a special filling of the Spirit subsequent to conversion. Elsewhere, the New Testament teaches that the Holy Spirit produces such love in all who are regenerate (*e.g.* Gal. 5:22). John 17 suggests that the Spirit uses the teaching about God that Jesus imparts to achieve this end.

According to John 3:1–16, the regenerating work of the Spirit is to bring people to faith in Jesus, enabling them to 'see' and 'enter' the kingdom of God and have eternal life. Put another way, that means knowing the only true God and Jesus Christ as the one he has sent (17:3). The Spirit who brings people to a true knowledge of God through the gospel will also bring about practical expressions of that relationship with God in the lives of Jesus' followers.

Conclusion

God is holy and those who belong to him must share in his holiness. But how does this happen for the followers of Jesus?

His prayer in John 17 stresses that God's word has sanctifying power. Even those who know themselves to be God's holy people under the Mosaic Covenant are challenged by Jesus' teaching to know God and share in his holiness in a new way.

At the heart of the revelation that Jesus brings is the proclamation of God's redemptive achievement in the death of his Son. In his death, Jesus demonstrates the love which God has for the world and which he desires to see reflected in the life of his people. With the gospel message about Jesus and his work, God imparts his Spirit to us and binds us to himself in love. That same word keeps us in holiness and love, enabling us to share in his mission to the world.

The teaching of Hebrews: sanctified by the self-offering of Christ

Hebrews offers an interesting parallel to John's perspective on the sanctification of the Son of God (Heb. 10:5–10). More than any other New Testament book, this 'word of exhortation' (13:22) also has much to say about the sanctification of believers, using transformed cultic terms. The writer clearly relates the sanctification of believers to Old Testament teaching, making that the framework in which to understand the theme.[11]

The self-sanctification of the Saviour

Hebrews tells us that, when Christ came into the world, he took upon himself the task of fulfilling the plan of God, as described in Psalm 40:6–8:

> Sacrifices and offerings you have not desired,
>   but a body you have prepared for me;
> in burnt offerings and sin offerings
>   you have taken no pleasure (Heb. 10:5–7).

Four technical terms are used here to describe the different types of sacrifice commanded by the Mosaic law. According to the psalmist, the whole system was designed to encourage and make possible *the willing self-offering of the people to God*, as indicated by the words, 'but a body you have prepared for me'.[12] Israel failed to realize this ideal of obedience and consecration to God. In the body that was 'prepared' for him,

33

however, the Son of God lived a life of perfect obedience to the Father, culminating in his death as an unblemished sacrifice for sins (cf. 4:15; 7:26–27; 9:14).

Jesus came to set aside the ancient sacrificial system by expressing the obedience which was always the intention behind the rituals (10:8–9). Finding the Father's will in Scripture, he was able to say with the psalmist, ' "I have come to do your will O God" (in the scroll of the book it is written of me)' (10:7). His complete self-consecration to God brought about his death, making possible a consecration of God's people in a way that had not occurred before. By the will of the Father, revealed in Scripture and carried out by the Son, Hebrews proclaims that 'we have been sanctified through the offering of the body of Jesus Christ once for all' (10:10). Believers are sanctified because of his definitive sanctification, 'once for all' (Gk. *ephapax*) in death.[13] Jesus is 'the sanctifier' of the people of the New Covenant (2:11, Gk. *ho hagiazōn*), because he was perfected 'through sufferings' (2:10). As such, he fulfils the role of the God of Israel under the Old Covenant (*e.g.* Ex. 31:13; Lv. 20:8; 21:15; 22:9, 16, 32).

Sanctification and the New Covenant

The notion that God sanctifies or consecrates a people to himself through Jesus' once-for-all sacrifice for sins is stressed by the words 'we have been sanctified' in Hebrews 10:10 (Gk. *hēgiasmenoi esmen*). The Greek periphrastic perfect points to a state or condition made possible by the self-offering of Christ in death. No further sacrifices or rituals are required to keep us in that sanctified condition.

The preceding context suggests that this involves a once-for-all cleansing from sin that the law of Moses could not provide (10:1–4). As in Old Testament teaching, purification and sanctification are closely related in the argument of Hebrews (cf. 9:13–14). Purification is the basis of sanctification. By his sovereign action in Christ, God sets apart and binds to himself those who have been purified from the defilement of sin. This objective, consecrating work of God has profound implications for the attitude and behaviour of those who believe.

In 10:11–18, the writer goes on to indicate that Jesus' perfect sin-offering inaugurates the New Covenant promised in Jeremiah 31:31–34. Under the terms of that covenant, God writes his law in the hearts and minds of all his people, enabling them to know him and serve him in a new way. Such dedication to God is made possible by the sacrifice which allows him to 'remember their sins and their lawless deeds no more' (*cf.* 10:17–18). As in Jeremiah's promise, so in Hebrews, a once-for-all forgiveness of sins is the basis of a new commitment to God on the part of his people.

Hebrews 10:10–18 suggests that the verb 'to sanctify' is primarily employed in a *covenantal* sense. Christ's sacrifice binds men and women to God in a new relationship of heart-obedience. The covenantal dimension is highlighted again in 10:29, where we are told that the readers were sanctified by 'the blood of the covenant'.[14] The writer recalls the language of Exodus 24:1–8, where the relationship between God and Israel was confirmed as Moses poured 'the blood of the covenant' on the altar and on the representatives of the people gathered with him on Mount Sinai. Hebrews 9:18–21 actually speaks about the first covenant being 'inaugurated' by Moses on this occasion. By implication, the New Covenant was inaugurated by the shedding of Jesus' blood. This also appears to be the message of 13:12, where we are told that he suffered outside Jerusalem, 'to sanctify the people by his own blood'.

The *cultic* dimension to the sanctifying work of Christ is more specifically developed in other passages. Those who come to him as 'the mediator of a new covenant' and trust in the cleansing power of his 'sprinkled blood' experience the benefits of his sanctifying death (12:24; *cf.* 9:13–14; 10:19–22). As the eternal high priest 'according to the order of Melchizedek', Jesus offered himself as a holy, blameless and undefiled sacrifice for sins (7:17–28). He entered once for all into the heavenly sanctuary for us, having obtained 'eternal redemption' (9:12). By the single offering of himself in death, 'he has perfected for all time those who are sanctified' (10:14).

The present participle in this last verse (Gk. *tous hagiazome-nous*, 'those who are sanctified') does not imply progressive sanctification in terms of moral progress. As in 2:11 (Gk. *hoi hagiazomenoi*), the sanctified are identified in a timeless and general way as the particular group within humanity that benefits from the sanctifying and perfecting work of Christ. What Christ achieved once and for all by his suffering and death must be conveyed and applied successively to everyone who is brought to faith. If the verb 'to sanctify' is used elsewhere in Hebrews in a covenantal and transformed cultic sense, it must be similarly understood in this context.[15]

Sanctification and perfection

In 10:14, the writer speaks about being 'perfected for all time' (Gk. *teteleiōken eis to diēnekes*). The perfection about which the writer speaks is not moral. In several contexts it is closely linked with the concept of drawing near to God, which suggests that we are perfected as 'worshippers' through the high-priestly ministry of Christ. Although Israel under the Old Covenant was able to draw near to God through the mediation of priests and the operation of the sacrificial system, the people were not 'perfected' in their approach to God (*cf.* 7:11; 10:1–2). However, with Jesus, 'a better hope' has been introduced by which we may draw near to him (7:19; 10:14).

This better hope is based on the 'better covenant', which has been enacted through 'better promises' (8:6). Here and now, we are 'qualified' to draw near to God with the certainty of sins forgiven and the confidence that we are in an eternally secure relationship with God (*cf.* 7:19; 9:9; 10:1–4, 14–23; 12:22–24).[16] Our hope is also to meet God face-to-face, in the glory of his eternal kingdom (*cf.* 2:10; 4:9–10; 12:14, 22–24; 13:14), and so perfection in Hebrews involves ultimate glorification. Even so, what we have yet to experience is only an unfolding of what has already been achieved for us by Christ's sacrifice. This is made clear by the use of the perfect tense in 10:14 ('he has perfected', Gk. *teteleiōken*).

Perfection is not synonymous with cleansing from sin, though it involves the latter as a most significant element. Perfection is also not synonymous with sanctification, though the two concepts are closely related. The terminology of perfection is used to proclaim the fulfilment or *consummation* of men and women in a permanent, direct and personal relationship with God.

Jesus' death brings about a cleansing from sin and a definitive consecration to God in the present. It also secures for us a share in the future that God has promised. We can draw near to God *now* with the directness and certainty that belong to the final state of his people (*cf.* 4:16; 10:19–22; 12:22–24). The perfecting of believers involves all of that. Our sanctification or consecration to God is only a part of the process of eschatological perfection, achieved through the perfecting of Christ (2:10; 5:9; 7:28). The way in which these concepts are related to one another and to the cross of Christ may be represented as follows:

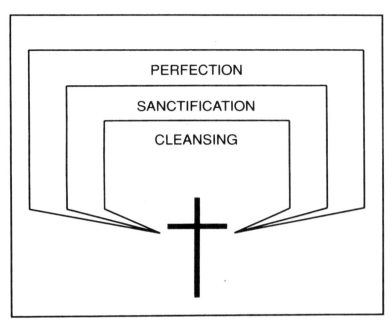

Sanctification and the conscience

Hebrews 9:13–14 exposes the effect of sanctification at the personal or subjective level. The writer first draws a contrast with the sanctification experienced under the Mosaic Covenant. Although Israel was made a holy people by being rescued from Egypt and brought together to live under God's word in the land that he promised, they remained a sinful and rebellious people. Rituals of purification were provided in the law for all forms of uncleanness, to 'sanctify' those who were defiled, so that they were made outwardly clean (9:13; lit. 'for the purification of the flesh'). Those who transgressed could be restored to fellowship with God in the sense that they were enabled to participate again in the worship of the community.

If animal blood purified and sanctified at a ceremonial level under the Old Covenant, the writer goes on to insist, 'how much more will the blood of Christ, who through the eternal Spirit offered himself without blemish to God, purify our conscience from dead works to worship the living God!' (9:14).

'The blood of Christ' is a way of speaking about his death as a sacrifice for sins. This was uniquely effective because 'he offered himself without blemish to God'. Once again the writer alludes to Jesus' life of perfect obedience to the Father, culminating in the cross (cf. 5:7–9; 7:26–27; 10:10). He offered himself 'through the eternal Spirit', which most likely refers to the power of the Holy Spirit upholding and maintaining him (cf. Is. 42:1). By contrast with the animal blood used in Old Testament sacrifices, the blood of Christ is powerful enough to 'purify our conscience from dead works to worship the living God'.

The writer has previously mentioned the need for repentance from 'dead works' (6:1), meaning that people should turn from everything that defiles the conscience and brings God's judgment.[17] But those who repent of dead works need to be cleansed from defilement *at the level of the conscience or 'the heart'* (contrast 9:9 with 9:14; 10:22), if they are to serve God effectively.

As in the Old Testament, 'the heart' in Hebrews is 'the centre of life and the epitome of the person' (Jacob 1974: 626–627),[18] the seat of rationality, faith, emotion and will (cf. 3:8, 10, 12, 15; 4:7, 12; 8:10; 10:16; 13:9). In 10:22 the writer says it is possible to draw near to God through Christ 'with a true heart in full assurance of faith'. This suggests:

> . . . a heart which fulfils the ideal office of the heart . . .
> a heart which expresses completely the devotion of the person to God. There is no divided allegiance: no reserve of feeling (Westcott 1914: 324).

Here the writer proclaims the fulfilment of God's promise to change the heart of his people (Je. 31:33; Ezk. 36:26–27 and parallels). This is made possible by the sacrifice which provides ultimate cleansing (Je. 31:34; Ezk. 36:25), expressed in Hebrews 10:22 in terms of 'hearts sprinkled clean from an evil conscience'.

There is no simple equation of heart and conscience here, although they are closely related. It is 'consciousness of sin' (10:2, Gk. *syneidēsis hamartiōn*) with respect to God that essentially concerns our writer. Just as the Old Testament speaks of the burdened, smiting heart (1 Sa. 24:5; 25:31; 2 Sa. 24:10; cf.

Ps. 51:3–11), so Hebrews speaks of a heart with 'an evil conscience', meaning a heart that is aware of God's command and authority and of having offended against these. Certainly, conscience can bear witness to the holiness and sincerity of one's motives in a positive sense (13:18, 'we have a clear conscience'). But the writer is fundamentally concerned with conscience as a register of guilt before God – with *the accusing conscience*.

The purpose of ritual cleansing in the Old Testament was that the people might be consecrated again to God's service. But the worshippers could not be perfected with respect to their consciences (9:9) and so they were sanctified only in a limited way (9:13). The New Covenant promise of a renewed 'heart' is fulfilled when people are set free from the burden of unforgiven sins through trusting in the effectiveness of Christ's sacrifice (9:14; 10:22). They are thus renewed in faith and sincerity towards God. Only the cleansing provided by Christ can definitively free us to worship or serve the living God (9:14, Gk. *latreuein*) in a way that pleases him and truly honours him.

Such worship cannot be restricted to prayer and praise, important though these activities may be in a genuine relationship with God. From the argument in 12:28 – 13:16, it is clear that we are to worship God by faithful obedience and service in every aspect of our lives.[19] Such a radical re-orientation of heart and life can only come about when people are moved by gratitude for receiving the benefits of the gospel. Faith leads to gratitude and 'by this means' (Gk. *di' hēs*) we offer to God 'acceptable worship with reverence and awe' (12:28, Gk. *latreuein*).

Conclusion

The sanctifying work of Christ in Hebrews has its *inward* as well as its *outward* aspects. His saving work brings about a cleansing and consecration to God that is viewed in transformed covenantal and cultic terms. When the message about his completed and eternally effective work is applied to the heart or conscience of believers, it brings about an inner conviction of forgiveness, acceptance and hope. A life of dedicated service or worship results. Consecration as a human response is made possible by God's initiative through his Son, cleansing us and consecrating us to himself for eternity.

Hebrews has nothing to say about the role of the Holy Spirit in this process. But the writer clearly sets forth a dynamic view of *the word of God* in 4:1–13. We may therefore conclude that he envisaged the gospel message about Jesus' high-priestly work having a transforming effect in the lives of those who believe it. When the sanctifying work of Jesus is proclaimed and believed, God changes our hearts and binds us to himself as children of the New Covenant.

The teaching of 1 Corinthians: sanctification, conversion and church membership

We turn now to another New Testament book where the theme of sanctification is critical to the argument. In Paul's first letter to the Corinthians, as in Hebrews, the emphasis is on God's sanctifying activity in Christ. Sanctification means being appropriated by God and dedicated to him by the saving work of his Son. The terminology is associated with the beginning of the Christian life and highlights the corporate dimension to sanctification in Paul's thinking. Sanctification has to do with the identity and status of those who are 'in Christ'. It also points to the lifestyle that is consistent with God's calling.

God's holy people

The apostle begins this complex letter by identifying his readers as 'those who are sanctified in Christ Jesus, called to be saints, together with all those who in every place call on the name of our Lord Jesus Christ, both their Lord and ours' (1 Cor. 1:2). As 'the church of God in Corinth' they belong to *God*, not to any of their teachers or leaders (*cf.* 3:9, 21–23). In ordinary Greek usage the term *ekklēsia* ('church') was applied to any sort of assembly for secular or religious purposes. But Paul's point is that the Corinthian Christians are 'the assembly belonging exclusively to the one true and living God'.[20]

The next clause, 'to those sanctified in Christ' (Gk. *hēgiasmenois en Christō*), amplifies what it means to be God's church. The Corinthian Christians were a holy and distinct people in that corrupt and godless city. This was so because of God's initiative, drawing them into an exclusive relationship with himself.[21] What he had done for them 'in Christ Jesus' had made them part of his eschatological community. Here the perfect passive participle 'sanctified' should be understood as another way of speaking about *their conversion and incorporation into Christ.* It can hardly refer to their holiness of character or conduct, since Paul spends much time in this letter challenging their values and their behaviour, calling them to holiness in an ethical sense. He does this on the basis that they are already sanctified in a relational sense, but need to express that sanctification in lifestyle.

Paul also reminds the Corinthians that they were 'called to be saints' (Gk. *klētois hagiois, cf.* Rom. 1:7). The adjective 'holy' in Greek (*hagios*) comes from the same root as the verb 'to consecrate, sanctify or make holy'. So the designation 'holy ones' or 'saints' is a shorthand way of referring to those who have been sanctified in Christ. The term has its origin in Old Testament descriptions of Israel as 'a holy nation' or 'holy people', chosen, called and set apart for God by the great exodus redemption (*e.g.* Ex. 19:5–6; Dt. 7:6; 26:19; Je. 2:3). It was later used more narrowly to describe the elect in Israel who would share in the blessings of the messianic kingdom (*e.g.* Dn. 7:18–27; Pss. Sol. 17; Qumran).[22]

Paul never again uses the full expression 'to those sanctified in Christ Jesus' in the opening address of his letters. Apparently, he wanted to emphasize this concept in writing to the Corinthians. 'Saints' becomes his regular way of describing Christians in general (*e.g.* Rom. 1:7; 8:27; 2 Cor. 1:1; Eph. 1:1; Phil. 1:1; Col. 1:2), though he sometimes refers specifically to the believers in Judea in this way (*e.g.* Rom. 15:25–26, 31; 1 Cor. 16:1; 2 Cor. 8:4; 9:1, 12). This title of dignity was peculiarly applicable to the primitive Jewish church, whom God had preserved and sanctified to be the channel of his light and life for the whole world. As the first Jewish believers received the gospel and proclaimed it to the nations, Gentiles were brought to share in the inheritance of 'the saints' (*cf.* Col. 1:12; Eph. 2:17–22).[23]

It is one of the tragedies of church history that, in official as well as popular usage, the term 'saint' has become too narrowly identified with apostles or outstanding Christian leaders and exemplars. The notion that all Christians are saints by virtue of God's calling is obscured by this misleading practice.[24] If a particular individual's sanctity is celebrated, it suggests that personal holiness is in some way a departure from the norm. Worse still, it implies that sainthood is an achievement, not a gift. If someone says, 'She's a real saint,' it ought in truth to mean, 'She's a real Christian'!

The last clause of 1 Corinthians 1:2 indicates that those who are 'saints by God's call' will themselves 'call on the name of our Lord Jesus Christ'. This is more than a general description of prayer. In Romans 10:9–14, calling upon the name of the Lord involves confessing the resurrected Jesus as Lord and trusting in him for salvation (*cf.* Acts 2:21, 36–40; 9:14, 21; 22:16). Those who have genuinely turned to Christ continue to pray to him for help and deliverance, as they endure the struggles of the Christian life and await the return of their Saviour (*cf.* Lk. 18:7–8; Acts 4:29–30; 12:5; 1 Cor. 16:22; 2 Tim. 2:22).[25] Wherever people gather together to call upon Christ as Lord and Saviour ('both their Lord and ours'), the church of God is manifested.

So Paul's opening address to the Corinthians stresses that those who truly belong to 'the church of God' have been sanctified in Christ and are therefore 'the saints' of the New Covenant. They have been called and appropriated by God, to be exclusively devoted to him and to his service. They demonstrate the reality of that sanctification by continuing to call upon Jesus Christ as Lord.

A new status in Christ

The theme of sanctification emerges again in 1 Corinthians 1:30, where Paul writes that Jesus became for us 'wisdom from God, and righteousness and sanctification and redemption'. Here the noun 'sanctification' is used as one of three metaphors to explain how God has made Jesus *the wisdom that leads to eternal salvation* (*cf.* 1:18–25). We cannot know God better or experience a deeper spirituality by seeking wisdom for ourselves. Against such misunderstandings at Corinth, Paul insists that Christ crucified has become the wisdom of God for us, historically and objectively. He is the embodiment of God's wise plan for us. More precisely, he is the ultimate expression of God's wisdom in the sense that he became 'righteousness, sanctification and redemption' for us.

With such terminology Paul is not describing a sequence by which God justifies, then sanctifies, then redeems us.[26] Rather, he draws on three different but related strands of Old Testament thought to describe the same reality, namely our status or standing with God through Jesus Christ (*cf.* 6:11).

'Righteousness' or 'justification' (Gk. *dikaiosynē*) is 'not so much an ethical term here as it is forensic, and highlights the

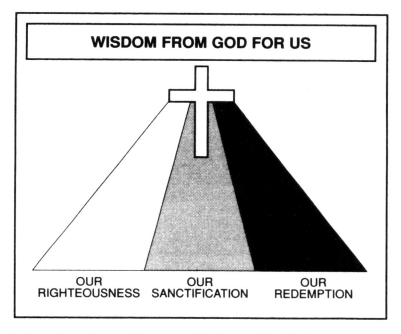

WISDOM FROM GOD FOR US

| OUR | OUR | OUR |
| RIGHTEOUSNESS | SANCTIFICATION | REDEMPTION |

believer's undeserved stance of right standing before God' (Fee 1987: 86).[27] 'Redemption' (Gk. *apolytrōsis*) is a metaphor from slavery, with special significance in biblical history because of the deliverance of Israel from captivity in Egypt and the later redemption from captivity in Babylon. Paul uses the language of redemption with reference to deliverance from the power of sin and its consequences through the death of Jesus (*e.g.* Rom. 3:24; Col. 1:14). The positive consequence of redemption is that we now belong exclusively to God. A related term is used when Paul tells the Corinthians, 'you were *bought* with a price; therefore glorify God in your body' (1 Cor. 6:20, Gk. *ēgorasthēte*). The price of such redemption was nothing less than the death of the Messiah, the Son of God.

Between the forensic imagery of justification and the concept of deliverance from slavery, Paul places the metaphor of sanctification. He uses the noun *hagiasmos*, meaning 'holiness' or 'sanctification', which clearly derives from the verb *hagiazein* ('to sanctify, make holy, consecrate'). It is sometimes argued that this noun, by its form and usage, emphasizes 'the moral element' (Procksch 1964: 113).[28] But the sanctification in view here is not a process of moral change. The context is about belonging to God and being given a holy status. The focus is on God's saving activity, not on our response.

Paul has addressed the Corinthians as 'those who are sanctified in Christ Jesus' (1:2) and has gone on to stress that Christ crucified is 'the wisdom of God' by which they are saved (1:18–25). Paradoxically, God has drawn to himself not many who were wise by human standards, not many who were powerful, not many of noble birth (1:26–29)! So the primary reference in 1:30 is to the work of Christ in giving them a new standing with God by means of his death.

Jesus delivers us from the dominion of sin and death (redemption). By his righteousness he also makes it possible for us to be counted righteous by God (justification). At the same time, he establishes us in a distinct and exclusive relationship with the Holy One (sanctification). In the great Christological statement of 1 Corinthians 1:30, redemption, justification and sanctification are overlapping, but distinct theological concepts.[29] This judgment is confirmed by the argument in 1 Corinthians 6:11.

A status that brings change

In the opening verses of 1 Corinthians 6, the apostle criticizes those members of the church who were taking one another before the public courts for the settlement of private disputes (6:1–8). Condemning the one who did the cheating in the first place, Paul proceeds to warn the congregation as a whole that those who do such things are in danger of forfeiting the kingdom of God (6:9–10). In the process, he makes it clear that at least some of them had been 'fornicators, idolaters, adulterers, male prostitutes, sodomites, thieves, the greedy, drunkards, revilers, robbers'. He implies that professing Christians who persist in such behaviour show themselves to be amongst those who will not inherit God's kingdom! But Paul cannot leave the matter there, especially since his argument might suggest that his readers were still among 'the wicked'.

'This is what some of you used to be', he affirms. 'But you were washed, you were sanctified, you were justified in the name of the Lord Jesus Christ and in the Spirit of our God' (6:11). His overall meaning is this: 'Your own conversion, effected by God through the work of Christ and the Spirit, is what has removed you from being amongst the wicked, who will not inherit the kingdom . . . Therefore, live out this new life in Christ and stop being like the wicked' (Fee 1987: 245).[30] As in 1:30, three metaphors are used to explain how the saving work of Christ can benefit us. Each aorist passive verb in Greek is preceded by the strong adversative 'but' (*alla*), though English translations rarely make this clear. Paul is offering three different descriptions of the same reality, rather than alluding to a process of being washed, then sanctified, and then justified.[31]

In the context, 'you were washed' (Gk. *apelousasthe*) implies a *cleansing from the filth of sin*. It is another way of talking about the effect of Christ's sacrifice on those who believe the gospel. If a baptismal reference is intended, Paul will be highlighting the spiritual cleansing which is sacramentally signified in baptism (*cf.* Eph. 5:26; Heb. 10:22).[32] The same verb is used in Acts 22:16, where Ananias says to Paul, 'Get up, be baptized, and have your sins washed away, calling on his name'. In the apostolic preaching, the offer of forgiveness is directly linked with repentance towards God and faith in Jesus as the Christ (*cf.* Acts 2:38; 3:19–20; 5:31; 10:43; 13:38–39). Baptism is not always explicitly mentioned in this connection, although it is regularly associated with commitment to Christ and the beginning of the Christian life.

When the apostle says 'you were justified' (Gk. *edikaiōthēte*), he employs the verb *dikaioun*, which comes from the same root as the noun *dikaiosynē* ('righteousness, justification') in 1:30. There has been much scholarly debate in recent times about the background and meaning of such terminology in Paul's writings. My own conclusion is that the forensic and declaratory elements of justification must still be considered as primary. Nevertheless, the notion of being *declared righteous by God* on the basis of Jesus' death must also be viewed within a covenantal or relational context. Paul is not speaking about a 'legal fiction'. The verb denotes:

> . . . God's powerful, cosmic and universal action in effecting a change in the situation between sinful humanity and God, by which God is able to acquit and vindicate believers, setting them in a right and faithful relation to himself (McGrath 1993: 518).[33]

What, then, is the particular contribution of the expression 'you were sanctified' (Gk. *hēgiasthēte*) to this context? Once again we have a verb (*hagiazein*, 'to sanctify') which corresponds with a noun (*hagiasmos*, 'holiness, sanctification') used in 1:30. This verb does not refer to a process of ethical development but highlights the fact that God claimed them as his own and made them members of his holy people. He turned them around and brought them to himself in faith and love. In ethical terms, however, such a separation from previous attachments and values has profound implications.

> Because of what God has done, the possibility of a new life is open to them; they are (in the language of v. 7) 'unleavened', and they must now purge out the old leaven and keep the Christian feast in sincerity and truth (Barrett 1971: 142).[34]

Paul's meaning is that:

> Having been once *justified*, they must not draw down upon themselves a new condemnation – that having been *sanctified*, they must not pollute themselves anew – that, having been *washed*, they must not disgrace themselves with new defilements, but, on the contrary, aim at purity, persevere in true holiness, and abominate their former pollutions (Calvin *Rom–Gal*: 1602).

It is fascinating to see how much Paul labours the point about the holy status of the Corinthians (1:1, 30; 6:11), as the basis of his appeal for holy living.

Where does the Holy Spirit fit into this picture? According to Paul, believers are washed, sanctified and justified 'in the name of the Lord Jesus Christ and in the Spirit of our God'. The first phrase recalls the description of Christians as those who 'call on the name of our Lord Jesus Christ' (1:2; *cf.* Rom. 10:9–14). Our new status depends upon the work of God in Christ and our relationship with him. This is initiated and maintained from a human point of view by trusting in the power of his 'name' and by continuing to call upon that name. The Spirit's work is to empower the preaching of the gospel about Jesus, enabling those who hear to understand and believe (2:4–5; cf. 2:6–16). So the Spirit is the means whereby God in the present age 'effects the work of Christ in the believer's life' (Fee 1994: 219).[35]

Furthermore, when we receive the Holy Spirit at conversion, we are formed into one body in Christ (12:13), a holy 'temple' in the Lord (3:16–17; cf. 2 Cor. 6:16–18; Eph. 2:21–22). From Paul's perspective, God is present and active among Christians in a way that surpasses his dealings with Israel under the Mosaic Covenant. He builds his church and sustains it in holiness and love, through the gifts and inspiration of the Spirit given to all his people (12:1–11; 14:1–40; cf. Gal. 5:16–26). So 'the fellowship of the Holy Spirit' (2 Cor. 13:14) is an important 'means of grace', by which God enables his people to live a sanctified life.

Noting the connection between sanctification and the work of the Spirit in 1 Corinthians 6:11, many theologians explain sanctification in terms of the renewal of our depraved nature by God's Spirit. There is undoubtedly a link between sanctification and regeneration, which will be explored more fully in later chapters. A profound change of attitude and behaviour on the part of the Corinthians is acknowledged by the apostle when he says 'this is what some of you used to be'. But the language of sanctification here refers quite specifically to the separation from a godless lifestyle that has come about by being attached to the Father through the redemptive work of the Son. Christ is the source of everything we obtain and this is communicated to us by the Spirit. The Holy Spirit not only brings the benefits of Christ's saving death to bear on the lives of believers at conversion but also 'effectively empowers them for life in the present' (Fee 1994: 130).[36]

Conclusion

What are the practical implications of the definitive or positional view of sanctification presented in this chapter? How could this teaching help a Christian struggling with temptation? What is the incentive for change? How might a person burdened with guilt because of disobedience and failure be encouraged by this approach?

I want to draw attention to four important consequences:

1. Our essential identity as Christians is formed by Christ and the gospel, not by our own personalities, backgrounds or

achievements. Through the death and resurrection of his Son, God has cleansed us from the guilt of sin and liberated us from its consequences and its control. He has set us in a right and faithful relation to himself, together with all who call upon the name of our Lord Jesus Christ. Drawing us into an exclusive relationship with himself in this way, he has made us his holy people, destined to serve him and please him for ever. Sanctification is about being possessed by God and expressing that distinctive and exclusive relationship by the way we live.

2. Although God calls upon us to express the fact that we have been sanctified by the way we live, our standing with him does not depend on the degree to which we live up to his expectations. It depends on his grace alone. Those who are bowed down by the pressure of temptation and an awareness of failure need to be reminded of the definitive, sanctifying work of God in Christ, by which he has established us as his holy people. On this basis, they should be urged to press on in hope and grasp again by faith the benefits of Christ's sacrifice. Approaching the exalted Lord with boldness, we may always receive mercy and find 'grace to help in time of need' (Heb. 4:16).

3. We must continue to see ourselves as God sees us in Christ.

> The moment sanctification is ejected from the temple of faith, and hence of justification, that moment justification by faith has become an initial stage on the pilgrim's journey, a supply-station which later becomes a pleasant memory (Berkouwer 1952: 21).

Someone who has struggled with homosexuality and found particular encouragement in the message of 1 Corinthians 6:9–11 expresses it this way:

> In Christ, God declares me to be 'righteous, washed, pure and set apart for him'. And yet there is nothing in my experience to suggest that these things could be so in and of myself. If I live by my own estimate of my life, I act accordingly. Alternatively, I can surrender my life to the lordship of Jesus and live by *God's* assessment of my life. So whose word will I live by? I am glad to live by God's word and the blessed release that it brings, looking by faith to him for who I am, looking in love to

my brothers for what I do. By his word, I am directed outward, never inward.

4. There is also a message here for Christians corporately. What will it mean to view one another as those already sanctified in Christ? Subsequent chapters will have much to say about this. Here I would simply draw attention to the fact that we quickly lose patience with one another when we are slow to change. For example, we are glad to receive new converts into our churches but sometimes reject them on the ground of continuing sin or because they fail to fit into the culture of the local church. This is particularly true for those who come in from the fringes of our society. But when we overwhelm people with conditions which they must fulfil to prove that they are making progress as Christians, we distort the gospel. We must learn to accept them as those already sanctified in Christ Jesus. The final shape of what they will be is in God's hands, and he will achieve his purpose in his own time and in his own way.

Chapter Three

Sanctified by word and Spirit

How is the sanctifying work of God in Christ applied to the life of believers? What part does the Holy Spirit play in this activity? Is there any ground for a 'second-blessing' approach to sanctification? Should we seek a special filling of the Spirit for effective growth in holiness? How is sanctification related to regeneration? What is the link between God's word and God's Spirit in sanctification? The following chapters consider such questions, which have been at the heart of debates across the centuries.

John Wesley (1703–91) was a key figure in the development of Protestant thinking in this area. Wesley believed that the Spirit's work of regeneration marked the beginning of a life-long process of sanctification. But he went on to propound a doctrine of 'entire sanctification' or 'perfection in love', to be experienced by Christians in this life. By this he meant:

> . . . a personal, definitive work of God's sanctifying grace by which the war within oneself might cease and the heart be fully released from rebellion into whole-hearted love for God and others (Dieter 1987: 17).[1]

This involved a total death to sin and a restoration of the image of God in the heart.

Wesley spoke of the need for a *crisis moment* of 'entire sanctification'. But he did not believe that this led to absolute perfection or sinlessness this side of the grave. He viewed such experiences as a means by which the Spirit might renew our zeal and enable us to *progess* in holiness. In other words, he looked for a process–crisis–process pattern of sanctification.

Subsequent developments of this doctrine brought many changes. As holiness movements multiplied in various parts of the world, many taught the need for a second crisis of faith, subsequent to justification, and the possibility of being entirely sanctified in this life. In time, an emphasis on eradication of the sinful nature among Wesleyan holiness advocates became more pronounced. There was a struggle with the Keswick higher-life movement over the question of whether the fullness of the Holy Spirit in the sanctified life freed one 'only from the dominion of sin or also from the presence of sin in the heart' (Dieter 1987: 42).[2] When the Pentecostal language of 'baptism with the Spirit' was drawn in to explain the dynamic of entire sanctification, another strand of holiness teaching began to develop.

Further evidence for what has been called positional or definitive sanctification in Christ is offered in this chapter. But the way in which such teaching is meant to promote practical holiness is also explored. Although many writers and preachers have been preoccupied with the question of *individual* growth in holiness, this chapter confirms the view that the sanctity of the church as the community of God's people is also a concern of the New Testament.

Sanctified by the washing of water with the word

Ephesians 5:25–27 has several important links with passages previously explored. Christ's word is shown to be the means by which he applies the sanctifying benefit of his death to us. As in 1 Corinthians, the corporate dimension of sanctification is stressed.[3] The novel element here is that the church is sanctified or devoted to Christ by the 'washing' he provides, suggesting a closer link between sanctification and cleansing than in 1 Corinthians. We are also shown how Christ's sanctifying work prepares us to meet him in glory. All this is in the context of demonstrating how the Saviour's love for his church is a pattern for a husband's love of his wife:

> Husbands, love your wives, just as Christ loved the church and gave himself up for her, in order to make her holy by cleansing her with the washing of water by the word, so as to present the church to himself in splendor, without a spot or wrinkle or anything of the kind – yes, so that she may be holy and without blemish (Eph. 5:25–27).

Sanctified by cleansing

It is natural to understand the verb 'to make holy' in Ephesians 5:26 (Gk. *hagiasē*) in the primary sense that I have suggested for other passages. Separation from everything unclean and evil is the negative dimension, and consecration to God and his will is the positive dimension. But there is a particular nuance here. Christ died to devote the church to *himself* in an exclusive and permanent relationship analogous to marriage. The NRSV translation 'to make her holy' is doubtless influenced by the fact that the adjective 'holy' occurs at the end of 5:27. This is a condition achieved by vital union with Christ through faith. There is no suggestion in the context that the sanctification of the church means making it progressively 'more holy'.

His sanctifying work is so closely linked to his 'cleansing' (Gk. *katharisas*) that we might translate, 'sanctify and cleanse her' (NRSV 'to make her holy by cleansing her').[4] Like the metaphor of 'washing' in 1 Corinthians 6:11, or 'cleansing' in Hebrews 9:13–14; 10:22, this may be a way of talking about the effect of God's forgiveness on those who believe the gospel (*cf.* Tit. 2:14; 3:5). Indeed, there is a link with the argument of Hebrews more generally here. Those whose sins are forgiven are set apart from all other attachments and are established on a new path of devotion to the one who cleansed them.

Such 'cleansing' is applied to believers 'by the washing of water with the word'. Some commentators relate this washing to the act of baptism and identify 'the word' with the candidate's confession of Christ. As in 1 Corinthians 6:11, however, Paul is more likely to be highlighting the spiritual cleansing which is represented in the water of baptism. Whether or not there is a baptismal allusion here,[5] 'the word' is most likely to be the gospel, which assures us of forgiveness and adoption as God's children. With this word of love, the Bridegroom binds himself to his 'bride', and brings the church to himself in love. In the gospel, the sacrifice of Christ is proclaimed and those who believe in it are set apart from the world and every other attachment to serve him in love (Eph. 5:1–2).

Prepared for glory

The ultimate purpose of Christ's sanctifying and purifying work is 'to present the church to himself in splendor, without a spot or wrinkle or anything of the kind . . . so that she may be holy and without blemish' (Eph. 5:27; *cf.* Col. 1:22). The time of this presentation to Christ is probably his second coming, since Paul speaks about the church being 'invested with glory' (NRSV 'in splendor', Gk. *endoxon*). As in Revelation 21:9–11, 'the bride' of Christ will be presented to him, 'having the glory of God'. This glory is 'the perfection of character with which the Lord has endowed her' (Bruce 1984: 389).[6]

My last chapter will explore the relationship between sanctification and glorification more thoroughly. Here it is important to note that everything in the Christian life, from beginning to end, is made possible by *Jesus' self-giving in death* (Eph. 5:25), previously described as 'a fragrant offering and sacrifice to God' (5:2). Only those who are sanctified by Christ *now* can be presented to him in glory *then*. Transformation is implied by the notion of glorification (*cf.* Rom. 8:29–30; 2 Cor. 3:18; 1 Jn. 3:2), the present work of the Spirit anticipating the ultimate transformation associated with the resurrection of our bodies. Glorification is God's gift to all who rely on the sanctifying death of his Son. He has already cleansed us from sin and set us on a new path of obedience. On the basis of what he has already done for us, he promises to bring us into his presence 'without a spot or wrinkle or anything of the kind'.

Conclusion

If God chose us in Christ before the foundation of the world 'to be holy and blameless before him in love' (Eph. 1:4), he accomplished that goal through the redemption he won for us in Christ. The benefit of his saving work is actually conveyed to us through the gospel, which declares that we are sanctified and cleansed. We stand before him already 'holy and blameless' in his sight and it is our Saviour's intention to keep us in holiness until we meet him as the glorified church. To that end, he 'nourishes' and 'tenderly cares' for us, 'because we are members of his body' (5:29–30).

The challenge of the wider context in Ephesians 4 – 6 is for those who enjoy that sanctified status to reflect it in a holy lifestyle. No greater encouragement could be provided for this than the assurance that Christ died to purify us from sin and sustain us as his holy people, until we meet him in the new creation.

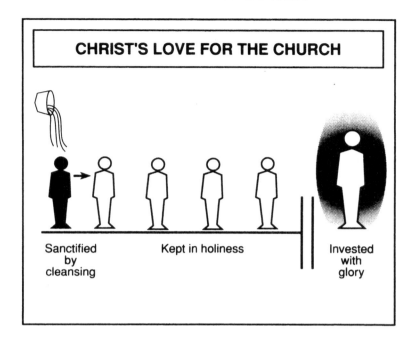

Sanctified by faith through the word

If the gospel is the instrument by which God consecrates us to himself through Christ, faith must be the means by which we receive that word and enjoy its benefits. The role of faith is stressed in the second of two passages in the Acts of the Apostles ' that speak of sanctification (Acts 26:17–18). The other passage makes it clear that the church is preserved in holiness by the gospel of God's grace (Acts 20:28–32). Both passages occur in speeches attributed to Paul and correlate well with the teaching of his letters.

Sanctified together

In Acts 26:18, Paul recounts to King Agrippa his commission from the risen Christ, to open the eyes of Jews and Gentiles, 'so that they may receive forgiveness of sins and a place among those who are sanctified by faith in me'. Sanctification here and in Acts 20:32 is not a stage or a process beyond the forgiveness of sins. The perfect passive participle in both texts (Gk. *hēgiasme-nois*) suggests that sanctification is the state or condition of those who receive God's forgiveness by trusting in Christ. Sanctification in this sense is simply received and experienced 'by faith'. Its outcome is a share in the destiny of God's holy people.

There is no ground here for divorcing sanctification from conversion or for propounding a crisis view of sanctification by faith as a 'second blessing'. By faith in the gospel, we continue to be united with Christ, which is the heart of sanctification. By faith, we rely on his promises and grasp the power of his Spirit, so that we can resist sin and live for God. This theme will be particularly developed in chapter five. Faith is 'not only a receptive organ but also an operative power' (Hoekema 1989: 196).[7] By its very nature, true faith produces spiritual fruit and sustains us as Christians until we share together in the inheritance promised to us.

The New Testament sometimes portrays that inheritance in terms of a transformed environment – as 'a new heaven and a new earth' (Rev. 21:1–8), as a redeemed creation (Rom. 8:18–23), or as an imperishable, undefiled and unfading possession (1 Pet. 1:4; cf. Heb. 9:15). But in Acts 20:32; 26:18 Paul speaks of an inheritance that is 'among those who are sanctified' (Gk. *en tois hēgiasmenois*).[8] The focus is on the people who will share eternity in God's presence. Our inheritance is to live for ever with all who are sanctified by God's grace.

Sanctified by the gospel of grace

In Acts 20:17–35, the apostle delivers a farewell speech to the elders of the church at Ephesus. As 'guardians' or 'overseers' of the flock of God (20:28), appointed by the Holy Spirit, they are challenged to 'shepherd the church of God that he obtained with the blood of his own Son' (NRSV).[9] Here the title 'church of God' (Gk. *ekklēsia tou theou*) recalls Paul's frequent description of Christian congregations in such terms.[10] When he speaks of God 'obtaining' or 'acquiring' the church (Gk. *peripoiein*), he uses Old Testament language associated with the establishment of Israel as the elect people of God (*e.g.* Ex. 19:6; Ps. 74:2 [LXX 73:2]; Is. 43:21; Mal. 3:17).[11] With the idea of the church being acquired by God, at the price of his Son's death, we have a parallel to the notion that we are sanctified as God's people through Jesus' redemptive work (*cf.* Jn. 17:17–19).

Paul's concern for the Ephesian church was that 'savage wolves' would come among them, 'not sparing the flock', some even arising from their own group, 'distorting the truth in order to entice the disciples to follow them' (Acts 20:29–30). This is reminiscent of Jesus' concern for his followers to be kept in holiness, one with the Father and the Son, through the work of the Holy Spirit (*cf.* Jn. 17:11–24). The apostle's primary emphasis is on preserving the holiness of the church by *keeping it from doctrinal error.* Moral and behavioural issues were doubtless at stake, but the integrity of the church as a believing community is his focus (*cf.* 1 Cor. 3:16–17).

Pointing the elders to the example of his own ministry in their midst (20:31), Paul commends or entrusts them to God and to 'the message of his grace'. This he describes as 'a message that is able to build you up and to give you the inheritance among all who are sanctified' (20:32). The 'message of his grace' (Gk. *tō logō tēs charitos autou*) is doubtless 'the message concerning his grace', since Paul has just mentioned his commission to testify to 'the gospel of the grace of God' (20:24).[12] Here is another way of speaking about the proclamation of the saving significance of Jesus' death. It is Jesus' death that actually saves and sanctifies but 'the message of his grace' conveys the benefits to believers. When that message is distorted, the holiness of the church is compromised because the basis of faith is obscured.

God uses the gospel of grace to 'build' the church (Gk. *oikodomein*), by adding new believers as 'living stones' to the spiritual temple he is constructing (*e.g.* 1 Cor. 3:9–10; Eph. 2:13–22; 1 Pet. 2:4–5). The apostolic message is also able to 'build up' the church in the sense of nurturing, uniting and strengthening believers to stand firm against false teaching, unfaithfulness and ungodliness (*e.g.* 2 Cor. 10:8; 12:19; 13:10; 1 Thes. 5:11; Eph. 4:11–16).[13] Finally, as we have seen, the message of God's grace is able to give believers the inheritance that God has bequeathed to them, by sustaining them in faith to the end.

Conclusion

Both passages in Acts highlight the human side to what is essentially a divine work. As the gospel is proclaimed and faith is elicited, people are brought together into a sanctified relationship with God through Jesus Christ. As the word of God is applied to everyday life and relationships, believers are built up and sustained in holiness, until they are brought to share in the inheritance that God has in store for them. Paul's exhortation in

Acts 20 suggests that teaching about our sanctified status in Christ is foundational for pastoral theology and practice. The church is precious to God and belongs exclusively to him. Christian leaders have a responsibility to protect it from everything that corrupts and compromises its holiness. Defending and propagating the biblical faith is an important dimension to the sanctified life.

Sanctified by the Holy Spirit

In chapter two, I argued that the Spirit's work in sanctification is to enable those who hear the gospel to understand, to believe and to be formed into one body in Christ, a holy temple in the Lord. This chapter has confirmed the view that God works through the apostolic word to sanctify or consecrate a people to himself. The Spirit's role in this divine activity will be further explicated as we examine more New Testament texts. What will also emerge is the Holy Spirit's role in motivating and directing a new life of obedience, hope and love, springing from faith in Jesus Christ. Further dimensions to the Spirit's work will be considered in later chapters.

An offering acceptable to God

At the conclusion of his letter to the Romans, Paul speaks of himself as 'a minister of Christ Jesus to the Gentiles in the priestly service of the gospel of God, so that the offering of the Gentiles may be acceptable, sanctified by the Holy Spirit' (Rom. 15:16). When he describes himself as discharging a 'priestly' ministry in the 'cult' of the gospel (Gk. *hierourgounta to euangelion*),[14] he does not mean that he is a mediator between his converts and God. Sacral terminology is used metaphorically to portray the ministry of preaching by which Paul enables people from every nation to offer themselves to God as an acceptable sacrifice.[15]

His claim that the offering of *the Gentiles* may be acceptable is quite remarkable, considering how much the ritual of the Old Testament was designed to express and maintain Israel's separation from the 'uncleanness' of the nations. But the distinction between clean and unclean, Jew and Gentile, had been broken down and abolished in Christ. It was no longer necessary for Gentiles to be circumcised or sanctified by any of the rituals provided in the Mosaic law. Because of the cross, a new way of approach to God had been provided for Jews and Gentiles together, 'in one Spirit' (Eph. 2:11–21; *cf.* Rom. 14:14, 20; 15:7–13).

The perfect passive participle in the expression 'sanctified by the Holy Spirit' (Rom. 15:16, Gk. *hēgiasmenē en pneumati hagiō*) suggests a state or condition brought about by their conversion or initiation into Christ (*cf.* Jn. 17:19; Acts 20:32; 26:18; 1 Cor. 1:2). When the Spirit brings people to faith through the preaching of the gospel, they are set apart from their unbelieving contemporaries and are bound together with other believers in an exclusive relationship with God.

Of course, the atoning sacrifice of Christ was at the heart of Paul's message (Rom. 3:23–25), and this is foundationally what makes the self-offering of Christians acceptable to God. Only because of Jesus' death can we be cleansed from sin and dedicated to his service. But gospel proclamation is the instrument by which the Holy Spirit 'associates believers with the sacrifice of the cross' (Leenhardt 1961: 368).[16]

The readers' reception of the Holy Spirit was a critical step in God's plan to create a sanctified 'offering' (Gk. *prosphora*) of Gentiles. This offering, however, concerned their ongoing lives and not simply their conversion. The language of Romans 15:16 recalls 12:1. There the challenge is given to those who are already Christians to present their bodies as 'a living sacrifice [Gk. *thysian zōsan*], holy and acceptable to God', which is the proper 'worship' of the messianic age.[17] By his presence in their lives, the Spirit who is holy enables God's people to live in a way that is pleasing to God.

A critical dimension to this new pattern of life is revealed in 12:2: 'Do not be conformed to this world, but be transformed by the renewing of your minds, so that you may discern what is the will of God – what is good and acceptable and perfect.' It is the Spirit's work to bring about renewal in Christians (*cf.* 7:6; 2 Cor. 3:18; Tit. 3:5), a subject examined more completely in the last chapter. Renewal of the mind makes it possible for us to go on discerning God's will and presenting ourselves for daily obedience, despite countless pressures to do otherwise.

The exhortations that follow in Romans 12 – 15 reveal the dimensions of a life consecrated to God, under the direction of the Holy Spirit. It involves effective ministry to one another within the body of Christ (12:3–13), maintaining love and forgiveness towards those outside the Christian community (12:14–21), acting responsibly with regard to civic authorities (13:1–7), living expectantly in the light of Christ's imminent return and demonstrating love (13:8–14), especially towards Christians with different opinions (14:1 – 15:13).

Romans 15 continues to reinforce the idea that the consecration of the Gentiles to God was directly related to Paul's preaching and the mighty works that accompanied it. Christ himself had been at work in the apostle's ministry, 'to win obedience from the Gentiles, by word and deed, by the power of signs and wonders, by the power of the Spirit of God' (15:18–19). Although his evangelistic work is included in this reference, it would seem again that the task of winning obedience included 'not only the believing reception of the gospel by the nations but also their constancy of Christian conduct' (Garlington 1990: 222).[18]

In Romans 1:5, Paul says that the goal of his ministry was to bring about 'the obedience of faith' among all the nations for the sake of Christ's name (*cf.* 16:26). I take it that he was seeking to encourage 'the obedience that springs from faith'.[19] This small phrase depicts God's design for a new humanity in Christ. Faith in Christ is a life-changing, sanctifying activity, with profound practical consequences. The Spirit, having sanctified God's people through belief in the gospel, continues to motivate and enable them to offer themselves in his service in a 'holy and acceptable' way.

Confirming God's call and election

In 2 Thessalonians 2:13–15, Paul links sanctification with the electing purpose of God and shows how such teaching is meant to be an encouragement to faithfulness and godly living, in the face of opposition and doubt. Resuming the note of thanksgiving with which he began the letter, Paul writes:

> But we must always give thanks to God for you, brothers and sisters beloved by the Lord, because God chose you [from the beginning] for salvation through sanctification by the Spirit and through belief in the truth. For this purpose he called you through our proclamation of the good news, so that you may obtain the glory of our Lord Jesus Christ (NRSV modified).[20]

Here we have 'a system of theology in miniature', covering the whole work of salvation from the eternal choice of God to the obtaining of glory in the world to come.[21] 'From the beginning', God chose a people for himself 'for salvation' (2 Thes. 2:13, Gk. *eis sōtērian*), which generally in Paul's writings means being rescued from divine condemnation and 'eternal destruction' (*cf.* 1:9–10; 2:9–12; Rom. 5:9; 1 Cor. 3:15; 5:5; Phil. 1:28; 1 Thes. 5:9).

God's purpose for his 'beloved' is also described more positively in terms of obtaining the glory of our Lord Jesus Christ (2:14, Gk. *eis peripoiēsin doxēs; cf.* Rom. 8:17–18, 30; 1 Cor. 15:43; Phil. 3:21; 1 Thes. 2:12; 2 Thes. 1:9–10). The means by which God achieves the salvation and glorification of his people is identified in the expression 'through sanctification by the Spirit and through belief in the truth' (2:13). Two co-ordinate activities are linked by the one preposition in Greek (Gk. *en hagiasmō pneumatos kai pistei alētheias*).

The work of the Holy Spirit is to consecrate believers to God (Gk. *en hagiasmō pneumatos*).[22] This is linked with belief or faith in the truth (Gk. *kai pistei alētheias*). From 2:10 and 12, it appears that 'the truth' is the truth of the gospel, which delivers people from perishing and offers them eternal life.[23] This judgment is confirmed by the argument of 2:14, where it is declared that God's call is heard and responded to in the proclamation of the good news.

The order of the two phrases in 2:13 is unusual. Sanctification by the Spirit is mentioned first and then belief in the truth. This suggests that Paul is using the terminology of sanctification to refer to the Spirit's definitive work in initiating a relationship with God (*cf.* 1 Cor. 6:11). The apostle's point would be that *belief in the truth comes by God's enabling.* 'Behind the will to believe is the consecrating Spirit of God' (Frame 1912: 281–282).[24] Put another way, the readers are being assured of their election because they have been sanctified by the Spirit and enabled to trust in the gospel (*cf.* 1 Thes. 1:4–10).

Most commentators ignore the word order and assume from the use of holiness terminology in 1 Thessalonians 3:13; 4:3, 4, 7; 5:23 that a *process* of sanctification beyond conversion is in view here. If such a process is included in Paul's thinking, then it will be an extension of the consecrating work of the Spirit associated with gospel proclamation and conversion to Christ. In other words, the Spirit uses the word to bring believers back to their rightful owner and to stimulate them to express the practical implications of that relationship. If 'sanctification by the Spirit' is a process that begins at conversion and continues until believers obtain the glory of our Lord Jesus Christ, the logic of this verse is that 'belief in the truth' is not simply an initial act, but 'a continuing habit' (O'Brien 1977: 189), motivated and inspired by the Holy Spirit. Paul is keen to point out in both his letters to the Thessalonians that *belief in the truth* is the key to profound moral and behavioural change.

This outline of God's saving plan in 2 Thessalonians 2:13–14 was designed to encourage Paul's converts to stand firm and hold fast to what they had been taught (2:15). In the face of persecution and affliction, they needed to be comforted and strengthened 'in every good work and word', which is the point of Paul's prayer in 2:16–17 (*cf.* 1:11–12). Central to his reassurance about God's loving purpose for them (2:13–14) is the statement about the sanctifying work of the Holy Spirit. His presence in our lives, enabling faith and the works that flow from faith, is a sign of God's electing grace. It is also a guarantee of God's intention to fulfil his promises and keep us to the end (*cf.* 2 Cor. 1:21–2; Eph. 1:13–14).

Summarizing the evidence of the Pauline references examined in this and the previous chapter, we may say that sanctification is the work of the Holy Spirit, creating faith in Christ through the preaching of the gospel. This work unites us to Christ, who is the source of our sanctification because of his redemptive work. The gift of the Spirit brings us together with other believers into a dedicated and distinct relationship with the Father, united as one spiritual family and as a people for his own possession and use. The Spirit continues to use the word of God and the ministry of his people to one another to motivate and sustain them in a life that expresses their holy status and calling.

Sanctified for obedience

There are interesting parallels to Paul's teaching in 1 Peter, where the readers are addressed as those 'who have been chosen and destined by God the Father and sanctified by the Spirit to be obedient to Jesus Christ and to be sprinkled with his blood' (1:2 NRSV). To strengthen them in the face of trial and to encourage them to lead godly lives, Peter emphasizes that they have a special relationship with God.[25]

The word 'chosen' refers to their election as his own distinct people (*cf.* 2:9, 'a chosen race'). The phrase 'destined by God the Father' (lit. 'according to the foreknowledge of God the Father') focuses on the basis of that election. Before they knew him, he knew them and decided to bring them to himself (*cf.* Rom. 8:29; 11:2). As in the Pauline letters, sanctification is associated with the notion of a divine calling and enabling to be the people of God.

'Sanctified by the Spirit' (Gk. *en hagiasmō pneumatos*) in 1 Peter 1:2 refers to a consecration 'wrought by the Spirit of God' (Michaels 1988: 11).[26] It is emphatically a divine act and an aspect of Christian initiation. Attaching believers to the Father by faith, the Spirit makes them 'aliens and exiles' (1:2; 2:11), not really at home in the world where they live. Their true home is the inheritance that is 'imperishable, undefiled, and unfading', made possible by the resurrection of Jesus Christ from the dead (1:3–4). Israel was consecrated to God as a holy nation by the exodus redemption from slavery in Egypt (Ex. 19:1–6). That status is now given to people of any race (1 Pet. 2:4–10), who are ransomed from a futile way of life 'with the precious blood of Christ' and have their faith and hope set on God because of the resurrection of his Son (1:18–21).

When Peter speaks about the way the gospel was brought to his readers, he mentions that the announcement of the human messengers was in association with, or 'by the Holy Spirit sent from heaven' (1:12; Gk. *(en) pneumati hagiō*). By implication, it is through the Spirit-empowered proclamation of the message about Jesus that God effects a consecration of people to himself. The Spirit is so closely tied to the word in Peter's thinking that regeneration takes place 'through the living and enduring word of God' (1:23–25).[27]

This suggests that regeneration and sanctification are two different ways of describing Christian initiation or conversion. But 'there is multiformity to that which occurs at the inception of the Christian life, and each facet must be accorded its own particularity' (Murray 1977: 285, note 2). Regeneration involves a new birth to faith, hope and love, made possible by the Holy Spirit. Sanctification has to do with the new status and orientation of those who belong to God and to one another as his people. Sanctification means having a new identity, with the obligation to live according to that identity. Regeneration, which is a definitive, life-transforming work of the Spirit at the beginning of the Christian life, has its continuation or extension in the process of renewal (*cf.* Eph. 4:22–24; Col. 3:9–11; Tit. 3:5–6). Sanctification has its continuation or extension in the life of holiness which the Spirit makes possible through faith in Christ. My concluding chapter will consider how these two different ways of viewing Christian experience are related together.

The purpose of the Spirit's sanctifying work is expressed in the third phrase of 1 Peter 1:2. Sanctification is, literally, 'for obedience and sprinkling with the blood of Jesus Christ'.[28] In 1:22 'obedience to the truth' is the means by which one is 'purified' or sanctified in the first place, which may be why 'obedience' is placed before 'sprinkling with the blood of Jesus Christ' in 1:2. Such obedience, which is another way of speaking about faith in Christ, is meant to be the ongoing characteristic of those who are sanctified. As 'obedient children',[29] Peter says to his readers, 'do not be conformed to the desires that you formerly had in ignorance' (1:14; *cf.* Rom. 12:1–2).

With this call for an absolute and perpetual divorce from the desires and practices of the old life comes a positive challenge to reflect the character of God in every sphere. 'As he who called you is holy, be holy yourselves in all your conduct; for it is written, "You shall be holy, for I am holy" ' (1:15–16; *cf.* Lv. 11:24; 19:2; 20:26). The rest of Peter's letter indicates what this means in practical terms. The motivation and direction for obedience is the holy *status* which God has given us by bringing us to himself and the holiness of his own *character*, revealed throughout Scripture but pre-eminently in his Son. God wants this holiness to be expressed by his people before an unbelieving world (2:11–12).

The linking of 'obedience' and 'sprinkling with the blood of Jesus Christ' in 1 Peter 1:2 recalls Exodus 24:3–8 and the sealing of the covenant between God and Israel at Mount Sinai (*cf.* Heb. 9:18–21). When the Israelites promised to obey all that the Lord commanded, Moses sprinkled sacrificial blood on the altar and on the people, signifying God's gracious acceptance of them and their obligation to be faithful to him. In Peter's argument, 'obedience' means accepting the gospel and its implications. 'Sprinkling with the blood of Jesus Christ' means being purified from sin and released from spiritual slavery by the power of his death (*cf.* Heb. 9:13–14).

Another way of expressing the call to live a consecrated or holy life is found in 1 Peter 3:14b-15a. Using the language of Isaiah 8:12–13, Peter's challenge is, 'Do not fear what they fear, and do not be intimidated, but in your hearts sanctify Christ as Lord' (Gk. *hagiasate*). The antidote to fear, when challenged or opposed for Christian commitment, is to acknowledge the holiness or distinctness of Christ as Lord *inwardly* ('in your hearts'). Closely connected with this is the challenge to acknowledge or declare that holiness *outwardly*. 'Always be ready to make your defense to anyone who demands from you an accounting for the hope that is in you', Peter says, and do that in the context of a life expressing Christ's lordship in every way (3:15b–16).[30]

Sanctified entirely

A wish-prayer in Paul's first letter to the Thessalonians is the only context in the New Testament where the language of entire sanctification is found.[31] However, it is not employed in the way that prominent holiness teachers have understood it. The prayer occurs at the end of the letter, gathering up the main pastoral exhortations of the preceding section (4:1 – 5:22). Paul's meaning is best revealed by this literal translation, which shows that he is using a form of synonymous parallelism:[32]

> May the God of peace
> sanctify you wholly (Gk. *holoteleis*);
> and in entirety (*holoklēron*) may your spirit and
> soul and body be preserved
> blamelessly (*amemptōs*) at the coming of our
> Lord Jesus Christ.
> The one who calls you is faithful, and he will do this.
> (1 Thes. 5:23–24)

This wish-prayer, like the one in 3:11–13, is ultimately oriented towards the return of Christ and has as its object the condition of believers at that decisive time.

In both prayers the apostle desires for the Thessalonians a perfection of holiness which goes far beyond and beneath merely outward ethical norms and behavior, and envisages their whole beings made ready to stand in the presence of God and Christ.[33]

Reference to 'the God of peace' (5:23) recalls the preceding context, in which the Thessalonians have been urged in various ways to be at peace among themselves (5:12–22). Indeed the whole letter has emphasized the need for unity and love amongst believers. So Paul addresses God as the source of harmony and wholeness, asking that he might sanctify them 'quite complete, quite undamaged' (Bauer *et al* 1979: 567).[34]

The apostle seeks 'the healthful reuniting of the church as a whole, including hopefully even those opponents who had brought divisiveness into the community' (Wiles 1974: 66.[35] 'Entire sanctification' in this context does not simply refer to an individual's spiritual development but has a corporate dimension. It describes God's goal for his people collectively, as believing communities. Christians should be praying in this way for the *congregations* to which they belong. Moreover, 'entire sanctification' is not a crisis moment in the process of Christian maturation, as Wesley and others proposed. Paul is praying in a summary and quite general way (Gk. *hagiasai*) for the complete expression in their lives together of what it means to be the holy people of God.

His second petition in 5:23 indicates that the completion of this divine work is associated with the return of Christ ('at the coming of our Lord Jesus Christ'). Furthermore, his request ('and in entirety may your spirit and soul and body be preserved blamelessly') picks up the emphasis of the earlier part of the chapter. Having challenged them to live sober and godly lives, because 'the day of the Lord' is near (5:1–11), Paul now prays for God to make that possible.

The terms 'spirit', 'soul' and 'body' are piled up to stress that God must keep every part of them blameless to the end. Such language is doubtless chosen for rhetorical purposes.[36] Paul particularly wanted to stress that salvation in Christ includes the sanctification of the body, which means treating the body as wholly for God's purposes now (*cf.* 1 Cor. 6:12–20) and praying for such holiness to be thoroughgoing in their lives to the end.[37]

He does not simply want his readers to be kept from sin. He

begs God to work out positively in their lives the full implications of that holiness which is his gift and calling to them (cf. 1 Thes. 4:1–8), and to keep them 'blamelessly' until the end. He does not want the day of judgment to discover them in disobedience or falling short of God's will for them. It is God who calls his people to salvation and this includes completion of the work of sanctification. So Paul concludes his prayer for the Thessalonians with the assurance that 'the one who calls you is faithful, and he will do this' (1 Thes. 5:24; cf. 1 Cor. 1:8–9; Phil. 1:6).

Sanctification here is not a second work of grace, though it clearly has a present and a future aspect. Paul primarily uses the verb 'to sanctify' with reference to Christian conversion and incorporation into the community of believers (Rom. 15:16; 1 Cor. 1:2; 6:11; Eph. 5:26). Being cleansed from sin and set apart for God's service, however, brings the obligation to reflect the holiness of God in every aspect of our lives. In 1 Thessalonians 5:23, the apostle speaks about the consummation of God's sanctifying work in a way that anticipates his later teaching about glorification (cf. Rom. 8:17, 29–30; 2 Cor. 3:18). His prayer encourages us to pray ourselves for God to fulfil his purpose for us.

Conclusion

In this chapter and the preceding one, I have demonstrated that sanctification is regularly linked with Christian initiation and the saving work of the Lord Jesus Christ. Moreover, there is a corporate focus to this teaching in the New Testament. When God sanctifies us as individuals, he establishes us as members of a holy fellowship, enabling us to play our part in maintaining and expressing the holiness of the church, in doctrine and lifestyle.

The benefits of sanctification are conveyed to those who respond to the gospel about Jesus in the power of the Holy Spirit. Sanctification involves forgiveness, cleansing, and a reorientation of life that results from trusting in Christ. God's purpose in bringing us to himself as a distinct and holy people is to glorify himself in the world. This happens as the character and will of the Holy One are reflected in the teaching, confession and lifestyle of 'the sanctified'. To this end, God is concerned to maintain them holy and blameless to the end. The presence of his Spirit amongst his people provides the energy and direction for this great work.

From one point of view, holiness means always starting afresh, acknowledging each day our status and calling as God's holy people and living it out.[38] The sanctified life involves dedicating ourselves again and again, 'as a living sacrifice, holy and acceptable to God' (Rom. 12:1), knowing that we can only do this because of his grace towards us in the Lord Jesus. In practical everyday terms, sanctification means living in gratitude for what God has already accomplished for us and promised us in Christ.

From another point of view, we are being shaped more and more by the totality of the grace coming to us in Jesus Christ – we are being 'glorified'. In this respect, the New Testament overturns all human-centred views of progress and growth.

> It is not that we are somehow moving toward the goal, but rather that the goal is moving closer and closer to us. This corresponds to the eschatological nature of the New Testament message. It is the coming of the kingdom upon us, not our coming closer to or building up the kingdom (Forde 1988: 29).

The practical consequence of this is to long for and pray for the complete expression of God's sanctifying work in our lives.

When Christians have moving experiences of renewal and re-dedication to the Lord and his service, they must learn to describe these in biblically appropriate terms. The New Testament consistently uses the language of sanctification to describe what it means to be 'in Christ'. To separate sanctification from redemption and conversion is inaccurate and unhelpful. In the final analysis, to separate 'entire sanctification' from the moment when we see God face to face is another way of distorting the teaching of the New Testament.

Chapter Four

Pursuing holiness

Introducing his classic work on holiness, Bishop J. C. Ryle (1816–1900) wrote these stirring words:

> True holiness does not consist merely of believing and feeling, but of doing and bearing, and a practical exhibition of active and passive grace. Our tongues, our tempers, our natural passions and inclinations – our conduct as parents and children, masters and servants, husbands and wives, rulers and subjects – our dress, our employment of time, our behaviour in business, our demeanour in sickness and health, in riches and poverty – all, all these are matters which are fully treated by inspired writers. They are not content with a general statement of what we should believe and feel, and how we are to have the roots of holiness planted in our hearts. They dig down lower. They go into particulars. They specify minutely what a holy man ought to do and to be in his own family, and by his own fireside, if he abides in Christ. I doubt whether this sort of teaching is sufficiently attended in the movement of the present day (Ryle 1952: x).

With insight and passion, Ryle attacked inadequate doctrines of sanctification and appealed for godliness in nineteenth-century England. His zeal for holiness and his manner of exposition were very much indebted to the Puritans of previous generations and his work continues to influence modern writers in that tradition.[1] The Puritans were particularly concerned to address those who had been raised with sound doctrine but lacked personal assurance of their relationship with God. They emphasized the need for 'a continuing cycle of endeavour and self-evaluation within the context of faith in the effectual work of God' (Hawkes 1990: 252). Their great concern was that no one might be content with self-deception.

I must confess to being both inspired and troubled by this approach. I warm to the teaching that sanctification is the invariable result of a union with Christ through faith. I wholeheartedly concur that it is the outcome and inseparable consequence of regeneration and a sure mark of God's election. I admit that genuine sanctification will always be seen and that, in certain respects, we have a part to play. I am moved by Ryle's challenges to please God and advance in holiness. But I have doubts about his presentation of the progressive aspect of sanctification.

Like many popular writers on this theme, Ryle believed that a person may 'climb from one step to another in holiness, and be far more sanctified at one period of his life than another' (1952: 20).[2] But is this the Bible's way of thinking? Scripture certainly envisages a process of spiritual maturation (*e.g.* 1 Cor. 3:1–4; Heb. 5:11 – 6:2) and urges progress in godliness (*e.g.* 1 Tim. 4:7–10, 15). There are also indications that we should increase and abound in love and holiness (*e.g.* 1 Thes. 4:1, 9–10). My problem is with Ryle's 'step' imagery and the implication that there is a graded form of progress that can lead to ever-increasing measures of holiness. Such an approach creates unrealistic expectations and is capable of producing guilt and despair in those who do not perceive the evidence of such progress in their lives.

Ryle emphasizes the sovereignty of God in the process of spiritual maturation but he has little to say about the way practical holiness emerges from definitive sanctification in Christ. Simply identifying sanctification with growth in holiness obscures the emphasis and balance of New Testament teaching. On the great day of judgment, it will certainly be 'utterly useless to plead that we believed in Christ, unless our faith has had some sanctifying effect, and been seen in our lives' (1952: 22–23).[3] But a focus on sanctification in terms of discernible moral progress may leave us in doubt about final acceptance at the bar of God.

Ryle argues that a lively *sense* of justification and an assurance of God's calling depend on the pursuit of holiness.[4] But this seems to put the cart before the horse. The New Testament emphasizes that we have been justified and sanctified by faith in Christ and his atoning death. That 'sense' of God's grace and calling which the Spirit enables through belief in the gospel is meant to be the motivation and direction for holiness of life.

Hebrews 12:14 is a key text in one of Ryle's chapters – 'pursue peace with everyone, and the holiness without which no one will see the Lord'. Like many other holiness teachers, he pays little attention to the context of this verse in the argument of Hebrews. So this chapter begins by examining that critical passage and goes on to investigate the call to holiness in other New Testament texts. To what extent are we urged by Scripture to progress in holiness and in what manner? How should we pray for one another in this regard? How might we expect God to answer our prayers?

Sharing God's holiness

To understand Hebrews 12:14, it is necessary to recall the writer's broad perspective on sanctification. It is also important to take note of the preceding context in Hebrews 12, with its claim that we cannot share in God's holiness apart from his working on us through disciplinary sufferings (12:10). What is the link between these passages? How can we pursue something that is God's gift to us?

Holiness as the gift of God

Hebrews 12 begins with the reminder that Christians are engaged in the same struggle that Jesus endured (12:1–4; *cf.* 10:32–34). Because of their commitment to God and the doing of his will, they experience physical suffering, social ostracism and abuse from their opponents. Such hardship is not a sign that God has lost control or abandoned his people. It is rather an expression of his fatherly *discipline* (12:5–7, Gk. *paideia*). We tend to think of discipline mainly in terms of chastisement and correction, but Scripture shows that in its widest sense discipline involves positive encouragement and training.[5] Applied to God, it refers to the whole nurturing process by which he 'brings up' his children and shapes them in the way he wants them to go.

Proverbs 3:11–12 is cited by the writer of Hebrews as an exhortation through which God continues to urge Christians, collectively and individually, not to 'make light' of his discipline. Suffering may provoke uncertainty and despair (*cf.* 10:35–39; 12:12–13), but we are not to 'lose heart' when trials seem to overwhelm us, remembering God's good and gracious purpose for us. God's beloved suffer 'precisely because God loves them, and they can take comfort from that fact' (Attridge 1989: 361).[6]

So Hebrews first describes the need for discipline in terms of God's fatherly care (12:7–8). Enduring trials for the sake of discipline should actually have the effect of proving the 'sonship' of God's children (*cf.* Rom. 8:17–30). Another dimension to God's training and correcting of his people is then highlighted in 12:9. We need to learn to respect and be subject to him in all circumstances as 'the Father of spirits'.[7] Bearing trials with patient and trusting submission is the only way to 'live' before him. In fact, the context suggests that submission to divine discipline is necessary for the enjoyment of life in the fullest sense, namely, life in God's presence for ever (12:1–2, 14, 28; *cf.* 10:38).

Human parenting may lack wisdom and be limited in its scope – 'they disciplined us for a short time as seemed best to them' (12:10a). But God's parenting of us is determined by his perfect wisdom and is motivated by his concern for our eternal welfare – God disciplines us 'for our good, in order that we may share his holiness' (12:10b; Gk. *tēs hagiotētos autou*). A rare Greek term for holiness here denotes the sanctity of God's character and life.[8] To share God's holiness is to enjoy life in his presence (*cf.* 12:9), transformed into his likeness (*cf.* 1 Jn. 3:2). In the final analysis, it is the same as being brought 'to glory' through Christ (Heb. 2:10). But even now, by faith, we experience some of the blessings of the age to come in anticipation (*cf.* 6:4–5; 12:22–24).

So Hebrews 12:9–10 suggests that, as we learn to submit to God's will in suffering, something of his holiness is reflected in our lives. We learn to acknowledge him as the Holy One, who is supreme over all, perfectly loving, wise and righteous. At the same time, he moulds and shapes us into the kind of people he wants us to be. Trials of various kinds are necessary for the formation of godly character (*cf.* Rom. 5:3–5; Jas. 1:2–4; 1 Pet. 1:6–9). But they are also necessary to keep Christians firm and faithful to the end, when by God's grace they will fully share his holiness.

Appealing to the human analogy again, the writer says: 'Now, discipline always seems painful rather than pleasant at the time, but later it yields the peaceful fruit of righteousness to those who have been trained by it' (12:11). The outcome of discipline is described as a harvest of peace and righteousness, using terms that are widely employed in Scripture to refer to 'the new age and future perfection' (Michel 1975: 446).[9] Once again, however, there is no need to restrict the enjoyment of such benefits to the future. God 'exercises' or 'trains' his people in the present, to produce in them the signs of a transformed and sanctified life.

The emphasis of the passage is on what God continues to do for us. Holiness, peace and righteousness are his gifts to us, as he enables us to go on trusting and obeying him. At the human level, faith is what sanctifies or makes the people of God different from all others. According to Hebrews 11, faith gives a different value system, with different priorities, leading to a profoundly different lifestyle. Hebrews 12 suggests that suffering nurtures faith, providing 'fertile soil for the cultivation of a righteous life, responsive to the will of God' (Bruce 1964: 361).

The response to this teaching about God's 'training' activity is finally expressed with language drawn from Isaiah 35:3 and Proverbs 4:26. 'Therefore lift your drooping hands and strengthen your weak knees, and make straight paths for your feet, so that what is lame may not be put out of joint, but rather be healed' (Heb. 12:12–13). The original recipients were encouraged to brace themselves for further conflict and trial. They were to keep running straight towards the goal that God had set for them (cf. 12:1–2), and not fall by the wayside in weariness.[10] But this struggle could not be viewed in exclusively individualistic terms. The challenge was for the *congregation* to endure and for special care to be given to the 'lame' in their midst. Even those who are spiritually weak may be 'healed' and kept on track by God, through the support and encouragement of other believers.

Pursuing peace and holiness

The exhortation in 12:14, to 'pursue peace with everyone, and the holiness without which no one will see the Lord', is pivotal to the argument of Hebrews 12. It picks up the note of 'peace' from 12:11 and the challenge of 12:12–13 to move *together* in the direction set by God. This prepares for the warning in 12:15–17 to care for any member of the church who may be in danger of committing apostasy. Although a different Greek word is used in 12:14, the note of 'holiness' from 12:10 is also picked up. The wonderful prospect of seeing God, which is another way of speaking about life in his presence, is highlighted. This motif is elaborated in 12:18–24, as the basis for a final challenge not to forfeit the grace of God and the blessings of the coming kingdom (12:25–29).

The present imperative, 'pursue' (12:14, Gk. *diōkete*), stresses the need for earnest, ongoing effort in response to the promises of God. It is not a call for the readers to achieve peace and sanctification by their own endeavours but to realize the practical benefit of what has been made available to them in Christ. Put another way, 'Christians must not become indifferent to the gifts they possess through the gospel' (Lane 1991: 449).[11]

'Peace' is the first goal to be actively pursued. This is not simply a state of mind but the total harmony that flows from a right relationship with God (*cf.* 7:2; 13:20; Rom. 1:7; 5:1).[12] The peace of God is given particular visibility in the love and commitment which Christians show to one another. Although it may be true that Christians are to seek peace with people in a whole range of circumstances, the most immediate application of the expression 'with all' in 12:15–17 is to the local church (*cf.* Rom. 14:19; 1 Pet. 3:11). Such peace is not to be cultivated now and again, when it is convenient for us, but 'it is to be striven for with the utmost zeal so that it is kept among us' (Calvin *Heb–Pet*: 195).

The same could be said for 'holiness' (12:14, Gk. *hagiasmos*), which is the second thing we are to follow after. Just as peace is a gift of God, the expression of which must be 'pursued' by Christians, so holiness is to be continually sought and expressed as a gift of God for the present. But this raises the fundamental question of how we are to understand and translate the Greek noun *hagiasmos* in this context.

The verb *hagiazein*, from which this noun is derived, is consistently employed in Hebrews to describe the consecration of believers through the death of Christ. We have been decisively and definitively cleansed and sanctified 'through the sacrifice of the body of Jesus Christ once for all' (NIV 10:10; *cf.* 9:13–14). The blood he shed for us is 'the blood of the covenant' that sanctifies us (10:29). Since he suffered outside the holy city of Jerusalem 'to make the people holy through his own blood' (NIV 13:12), his death is the means of consecration that replaces all others.

Such texts demonstrate that sanctification in Hebrews has to do with initiation into Christ, our consequent standing with God and the consecration of life that results. Logically, the noun *hagiasmos* refers to this sanctifying activity (so NASV Heb. 12:14, 'the sanctification without which no one will see the Lord'). If the Greek is translated 'holiness', it should be understood from the writer's use of the related verb that the allusion here is to a condition or quality of life resulting from the sanctifying work of Christ.[13]

The readers were to seek holiness as a practical expression of their sanctification in Christ, at the same time remembering the promise that God is disciplining his children so that they might 'share his holiness' (12:10, Gk. *hagiotēs*). This tension between the 'now' and the 'not yet' in sanctification will be more fully explored in the next chapter. From the perspective of Hebrews, since we are now 'holy partners in a heavenly calling' (3:1), we can expect God to be at work in our lives to manifest his holiness. By endurance and submission in suffering we pursue a significant pathway to transformation and change that God himself has prescribed. But in all this we are called to recognize that the ultimate experience of holiness awaits us in God's presence.

Those who are sanctified must especially reflect in their life together attitudes and behaviour that are consistent with their new situation in Christ. As the following passage suggests, we 'pursue' the peace and holiness of the believing community by nurturing and encouraging the faith and obedience of each member (12:15–17). Peace and holiness in the church are the signs of God's presence with us and his rule over us.[14]

We cannot add anything to the holiness God offers us in Christ. But the possibility of forfeiting the grace of God and missing out on the blessing of seeing him is powerfully expressed in 12:15–17 (*cf.* 6:4–8; 10:26–31). Esau spurned God's holiness and became a pattern of the arrogant unbelief that leads to rebellion. He is a warning to those who are preoccupied with self-gratification and who so easily turn their backs on God and his promises. 'Stubbornness, when it grows, produces the noxious fruit of apostasy, which is equivalent to excluding oneself from the grace of God' (Lane 1991: 453).[15]

So the challenge is to pursue practical expressions of the holiness or sanctification that is ours in Christ. Final salvation depends on it in the sense that a genuine knowledge of God will be demonstrated in a holy lifestyle (*cf.* 11:24–28). We particularly need to minister to those who may be spiritually careless and who may defile the holy character of the Christian fellowship by abandoning Christ and his people.

Drawing near to God

The crucial importance of pursuing holiness is underscored by the qualifying phrase 'without which no one will see the Lord'. Only those cleansed from sin and consecrated by the death of his Son can have access to God and live in his presence. But those who have been sanctified through Christ will demonstrate that fact by pursuing the values and characteristics of the One to whom they belong. Without such holiness, there remains only 'a fearful prospect of judgment, and a fury of fire that will consume the adversaries' (10:27). Apart from Christ and his sanctifying blood, 'It is a fearful thing to fall into the hands of the living God' (10:31).

Such teaching recalls the command to the Israelites at Mount Sinai to be ritually purified and consecrated, so that they could meet God without being consumed by his holiness (Ex. 19:10–25). Their sanctification, however, was designed to initiate and inspire a life of holiness in obedience to God's word (Ex. 20 – 24). They were not *made* holy by such obedience in the first place, but those who had been graciously ushered into his presence were to continue to recognize his holiness by their obedience. Judgment soon fell on those who made light of his demands (*e.g.* Ex. 32).

Hebrews 12:18–24 goes on to contrast Israel's terrifying encounter with God at Sinai and the approach of Christians to 'God the judge of all' in the heavenly Jerusalem. Jesus, 'the mediator of a new covenant' makes it possible for us to be purified, sanctified and perfected, because of his 'sprinkled blood'. We may continue to draw near to God in his heavenly sanctuary, with absolute confidence in Jesus and what he has achieved (4:14–16; 10:19–22), until we literally enter his presence and see him as he is. Yet even the wonderfully assuring picture of our participation in the heavenly assembly (12:22–24) is followed by a warning to go on heeding the voice of God (12:25–29). God's unshakeable kingdom is a gift to be received by faith and those who have truly received it will express their gratitude by offering to God 'acceptable worship with reverence and awe'.

Specific guidelines for a holy life, dedicated to the service or worship of God (12:28–29), are set out in the concluding chapter of Hebrews. Holy living has to do with such practical matters as entertaining strangers, visiting prisoners, being faithful in marriage, trusting God to provide material needs, imitating the faith of Christian leaders, not being carried away by strange teachings, doing good and sharing what you have with others.

In the light of Hebrews 12, the diagram on page 55 of the previous chapter may be modified as follows. Those who are cleansed and consecrated by Christ, and who look forward to sharing the perfection of holiness in his presence for ever, will pursue holiness as a lifestyle. As they seek the fulfilment of God's purposes, he produces in them the fruit of sanctification. The notion of being transformed into the likeness of Christ is not actually explored in Hebrews and will be discussed in the last chapter.

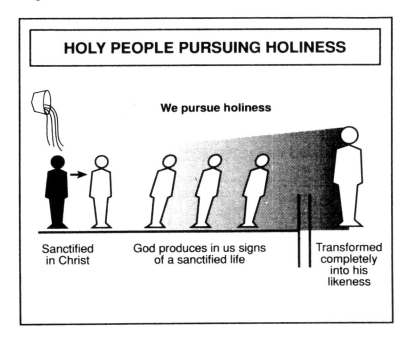

HOLY PEOPLE PURSUING HOLINESS

We pursue holiness

Sanctified in Christ

God produces in us signs of a sanctified life

Transformed completely into his likeness

Praying for one another

If holiness is both a gift and a calling in the lives of believers, how should we pray for one another? The 'wish-prayer' in

1 Thessalonians 3:11–13 gives some helpful clues. As the apostle intercedes for his converts, we learn what to pray so that holiness may be expressed and maintained in our own lives and in the lives of other Christians. It should be remembered that there is a somewhat similar wish-prayer in 1 Thessalonians 5:23–24, already examined at the end of the last chapter.

To increase and abound in love

Although Paul expresses great joy and confidence in the faith, hope and love of the Thessalonians, he assures them of his continuing prayer for them, asking that he might be able to see them again and 'restore whatever is lacking' in their faith (1 Thes. 3:6–10). Some indication of the instruction he thought they needed is given in 1 Thessalonians 4 – 5. Before he proceeds to exhort them, however, he amplifies his concern for them in this prayer:

> Now may our God and Father himself and our Lord Jesus direct our way to you. And may the Lord make you increase and abound in love for one another and for all, just as we abound in love for you. And may he so strengthen your hearts in holiness that you may be blameless before our God and Father at the coming of our Lord Jesus with all his saints (1 Thes. 3:11–13).

Only God the Father and the Lord Jesus could overcome the obstacles Paul experienced and make it possible for him to minister again to these new converts in person (3:11). Only the Lord could work within them the changes that were necessary for them to 'increase and abound in love for one another and for all' (3:12).

Paul commends them for their love three times in this letter (1:3; 3:6; 4:9–10), but he knows that the pressures they are undergoing from persecution have the potential for division and selfishness in their midst. So he prays for them using the verbs 'to increase' (Gk. *pleonasai*) and 'to abound' (Gk. *perisseusai*). Taken together, they imply a superabundance beyond imagination. He wants them to experience an extravagant increase in love, even as his love, as evangelist and pastor, has abounded for them. Such love cannot be confined to the Christian fellowship ('for one another'). In contrast with

78

Hebrews 12:14, love here must overflow 'for all', including those who persecute the church (*cf.* 5:15; Rom. 12:9–14, 17–21).

To be established blameless in holiness

The structure of Paul's prayer in Greek indicates that this increase in love is to be the means by which their hearts are, literally, 'established blameless in holiness before our God and Father, at the coming of our Lord Jesus with all his saints' (3:13).[16] In 2:4, we are told that 'God tests our hearts', and the same framework of judgment is intended in 3:13 (*cf.* 1 Cor. 4:5). As noted previously, the heart is the seat of understanding, affection and will in biblical teaching, 'the place where the hidden motives of life and conduct take shape' (Bruce 1983: 72). God must fortify us with love in the very centre of our being if we are to stand before him 'blameless in holiness' (Gk. *amemptous en hagiōsynē*).

The word for holiness here (*hagiōsynē*) is used on only two other occasions in the New Testament (Rom. 1:4; 2 Cor. 7:1), though the related noun *hagiotēs* in Hebrews 12:10 is doubtless a synonym. Both terms refer to *a quality of life and character*, arising from a relationship with the Holy One. In Paul's prayer, the key to this is love.

> As they stand before God now (1 Thes. 3:8), so they will stand before him in that day when all secrets will be revealed; if they are strengthened inwardly in love now, so they will be rendered blameless in holiness at the parousia (Wiles 1974: 62).

I argued in my last chapter that sanctification in Pauline teaching is the work of the Holy Spirit, uniting us by faith to Christ and to one another, through the preaching of the gospel. God then desires that the status of holiness which he gives us through the redemptive work of Christ should be expressed in a quality of life reflecting his character and will. For those who are genuinely consecrated to God, the goal can be nothing less than blamelessness in word and action (*cf.* Phil. 2:15). God himself is pure and blameless and he desires his children to reflect his character. Since the Spirit brings us together with other believers into a dedicated and distinct relationship with the Father, love for one another in the family of God will be a vital expression of true holiness. Moreover, love for those outside the Christian community will be a powerful revelation of the character of God to an unbelieving world.

No-one can be 'blameless in holiness' without the love that God's Spirit inspires and enables (cf. Rom. 5:5; Gal. 5:22–26). Where God's love is present and active, believers can stand firm for God and remain faithful and fruitful to the end. Put another way, love is (lit.) 'the bond that leads to perfection' (Col. 3:14, Gk. *syndesmos tēs teleiotētos*).[17] Paul's concern in his various letters is for his converts to take their part in building up the body of Christ in love, so that Christ's people might attain the perfection of his kingdom together.

The adjective 'blameless' (1 Thes. 3:13, Gk. *amemptos*) can be used to describe those who are pure and upright, not susceptible to any charge of wrong (*e.g.* Job 1:8; 22:3; Lk. 1:6). According to Paul's own testimony, however, it is possible to be observably blameless (Phil. 3:6, 'as to righteousness under the law'), but not in the end be pleasing to God.[18] Hence the importance of his prayer for that inner strengthening of the heart in love, which is the secret of true holiness. Blamelessness before God is closely linked with living in love, because love influences thinking, desires, motivation and behaviour.

Paul prays for his converts to manifest the integrity and purity of a life moved by the love of God. He asks for the love of the Thessalonians to increase and abound in the present so that their hearts might be found 'blameless in holiness' when Jesus returns to execute judgment. Indeed, he wants them to take their place in glory with all the 'holy ones' (Gk. *tōn hagiōn*, 3:13) that Jesus will bring with him.[19] This privilege is God's gracious gift for those whom he has chosen, called and sanctified (*cf.* 2 Thes. 2:13). But those who are genuinely sanctified by the Spirit of God will demonstrate their calling and status by seeking to lead a life 'worthy of God' (1 Thes. 1:12).[20] They will join with the apostle in praying as he does in 1 Thessalonians 3:12–13.

Love and holiness are two related ways of viewing the Christian life. Holiness will be pre-eminently expressed in love, and love will be the essential means by which holiness is maintained. Paul's prayer indicates that love must increase and abound, if believers are to persist in holiness. He does not actually pray for an increase in holiness here, even though he seeks their entire sanctification 'at the coming of our Lord Jesus

Christ' (5:23). In effect, holiness abounds when love abounds. But there is no suggestion that a second 'crisis of faith' can bring us to an immediate perfection in love or to a new level of spirituality where practical holiness becomes more attainable.

Pleasing God

Between the wish-prayers in 1 Thessalonians 3:11–13 and 5:23–24, Paul presents some critical teaching on practical holiness (4:1–8). In these chapters, he amplifies instructions given to them when he was with them and answers questions which they appear to have sent through Timothy. The opening verse of this section indicates that they had received, not only the saving message of the gospel (*cf.* 2:13), but also ethical guidelines ('how you ought to live and to please God', 4:1).[21] These instructions were given 'through the Lord Jesus' (4:2), that is, with his authority. The apostle acknowledges that the Thessalonians have been following his instructions, but wants them to do so 'more and more'.

Holiness as the essential will of God

Since 1 Thessalonians was written soon after Paul's first missionary journey, it probably contains the earliest occurrences of the noun *hagiasmos* in Christian literature. There are three possible ways that this term could be understood in 4:3:

1. God's will is the 'sanctification' of his people in the sense of their *progressive moral transformation.* But this is the least likely rendering in the context. The somewhat ambiguous meaning of *hagiasmos* in 4:3 is clarified by its use on two further occasions in this passage (4:4, 7), where the dynamic sense of 'progressive moral transformation' is inappropriate.

2. God's will is the 'sanctification' of his people in the sense of their *continuing consecration to his service.* With this reading, the message of 4:4 is that the human body belongs to the Lord and must be kept or controlled 'in sanctification and honour' (Gk. *en hagiasmō kai timē*).[22] Instead of dishonouring the body by inappropriate sexual behaviour, Christians are to glorify God by treating their bodies as 'consecrated' to his service. This is a vital way of recognizing and expressing the fact that we have been redeemed and dedicated to God, body, soul and spirit (*cf.* 1 Cor.

6:20; Rom. 12:1). Again, in 4:7 Christians are called to serve God as those who have already been 'sanctified' by his gracious initiative: 'for God did not call us to impurity but in sanctification'.[23]

3. God's will is the 'holiness' of his people in the sense that he calls us to *a totally different quality and character of life.* He wants us to live as those who are 'saints by calling' (*cf.* Rom. 1:7; 1 Cor. 1:2, Gk. *klētoi hagioi*), manifesting in daily life the practical implications of his sanctifying work, for us and in us. As a Jew, Paul regarded the will of God as the ultimate guide to behaviour. In line with Old Testament teaching, he therefore declares that the essential will of God is that his people should be holy (*cf.* Lv. 11:44–5; 19:2; 20:7; 1 Pet. 1:15–16).[24]

The following exposition of 1 Thessalonians 4:3–7 shows that 'holiness' is an appropriate rendering of *hagiasmos* in each case. But it must be acknowledged that 'sanctification' in the sense of consecration is also possible. Indeed, consecration to God and his service is the key to holiness of life in Paul's teaching.

Holiness and sexuality

The apostle first makes it clear that holiness must be exhibited in the sexual realm. 'Chastity is not the whole of sanctification, but it is an important element in it, and one which had to be specially stressed in the Greco-Roman world of that day' (Bruce 1983: 82).[25] Various forms of extra-marital sexual union were widely tolerated and some were even encouraged. Sexual indulgence was often associated with the practice of religious cults and there was no widespread public opinion to discourage immorality. It hardly needs to be pointed out that contemporary Christians find themselves in a similar ethical environment. But when the gospel is introduced into a culture it demands a new way of life in those who believe it.

In the pagan world of the first century, it was radical to claim that holiness must be expressed by abstaining from fornication (1 Thes. 4:3, Gk. *apechesthai apo tēs porneias*). Paul explains what he means by this in 1 Thes. 4:4–7, where it appears that any form of sexual relationship outside marriage is covered by the word *porneia*.[26] If our bodies belong to the Lord, we are no longer free to use them selfishly or in accordance with the accepted values of the time.

There are two basic principles in this connection, which the apostle later develops in 1 Corinthians. First, the body, which has been redeemed 'for the Lord', and which is now 'a temple of the Holy Spirit', cannot be united with a prostitute (1 Cor. 6:13–20). So believers are to 'shun fornication' (Gk. *pheugete tēn porneia*, 6:18). Second, when God gives the gift of marriage to a man and a woman, their bodies belong to one another. Husbands and wives should use their bodies exclusively for the benefit and pleasure of their spouse (7:3–4). In these passages, the notion of 'belonging', which is fundamental to the concept of holiness, is shown to be the basis of Paul's sexual ethic.

The charge to 'abstain from fornication' in 1 Thessalonians 4:3 is amplified in these terms: 'that each one of you know how to control your own body in holiness and honor, not with lustful passion, like the Gentiles who do not know God' (4:4–5).[27] Gaining control over one's body and refusing to use it for self-indulgence expresses a true knowledge of God and his will for human life (*cf.* Rom. 1:18–28). Those who have come to know God in Jesus Christ will treat their bodies as *his* property.

Some have argued that the apostle introduces a new subject in 4:6, warning against the exploitation of a 'brother' in the field of commerce.[28] It is certainly critical to see God's call for holiness extending to every sphere of life, not least to the factory, the shop and the office, where covetousness tempts us all to defraud or manipulate others. There are no compelling reasons, however, to conclude that Paul moves away from his focus on sexual matters in this verse. Indeed, the mention of 'impurity' (Gk. *akatharsia*) in 4:7 confirms that the subject of the preceding verse is sexual rather than commercial behaviour.

Paul warns against the *social consequences* of sexual indulgence in 4:6. Christians must beware of trespassing against brothers and sisters in Christ by behaving covetously (Gk. *pleonektein*). We must not only care about honouring God with our own bodies but also be concerned about injuring others.[29] By crossing forbidden sexual boundaries, we may enrich ourselves at someone else's expense. Husbands, parents, and other family members are all hurt when someone is seduced into an improper relationship. The Lord Jesus himself is 'an avenger in all these things' and will inflict the appropriate judgment on those who disregard his will (4:6b; *cf.* 2 Thes. 1:6–10).

The flow of the argument in 4:6–7 suggests that the coming judgment and God's initial calling of us 'in holiness' are to be the ground and motivation for holy living. God did not call us 'for impurity' but, by setting us apart for himself, he indicated his desire for us to live differently, as those who belong to him. The strength to live differently is experienced by those who know that they are loved and possessed by God.

Holiness as the demand of God's Spirit

A final reason for obeying God in sexual matters is introduced by the emphatic connecting word 'therefore' in 4:8 (Gk. *toigaroun*). 'Therefore whoever rejects this rejects not human authority but God, who also gives his Holy Spirit to you.' The apostle returns to the point made in 4:2, insisting that his instructions come with divine authority. Those who teach a more permissive policy or disregard Paul's words by their actions are setting aside the explicit will of God. Indeed, the Spirit he gives to Christians is the Spirit of *holiness*,[30] and nothing unholy can be tolerated in the lives of individuals or communities where the Holy Spirit dwells (*cf.* 1 Cor. 3:16–17; 6:19–20; 2 Cor. 6:14 – 7:1). As he puts it elsewhere, the Spirit is given to make it possible for God's people to exhibit the fruit of 'love, joy, peace, patience, kindness, generosity, faithfulness, gentleness and self-control' (Gal. 5:22–23).

Paul grounds his exhortation to holiness in 1 Thessalonians 4:8 by appealing to the fact of *God's continuous, sanctifying presence.*[31] His reference to the giving of God's Spirit specifically recalls the promise of Ezekiel 36:27 ('I will put my spirit within you, and make you follow my statutes and be careful to observe my ordinances'). Moving to a related theme in 4:9, Paul says, 'Now concerning brotherly love, you do not need to have anyone write to you, for you yourselves have been taught by God to love one another' (NRSV adapted). He notes how their love has been generously expressed, but urges them 'to do so more and more' (4:10). Here, the ground of his appeal is the fact that they have been 'taught by God' (Gk. *theodidaktoi este*), which is a way of proclaiming the fulfilment of Jeremiah 31:34 ('No longer shall they teach one another, or say to each other, "Know the LORD", for they shall all know me, from the least of them to the greatest').[32]

God is at work in the people of the New Covenant through the energizing and consecrating power of his Spirit (4:8), teaching and moulding them through his implanted word to conform to his will (4:9). Both verses imply that 'it is God's activity within the hearts of Christians that *impels* them to action' (Deidun 1981: 58).[33] God's holiness – what he essentially is – is present to us in the Holy Spirit. God's Spirit demands and makes possible the reflection of his holiness in the lives of his people. We must not resist his Spirit by unchaste or loveless behaviour, but rather 'abound' in love (Gk. *perisseuein*, 4:10), which effectively means abounding in holiness (*cf.* 4:1; 3:11–13).

Preserving the holiness of the church

In 2 Corinthians 7:1, Paul challenges his readers to cleanse themselves 'from every defilement of body and of spirit, making holiness perfect in the fear of God'. This verse forms the climax of a section beginning with the warning, 'Do not be mismatched with unbelievers' (6:14), and including a challenge to 'come out from them, and be separate' (6:17; *cf.* Is. 52:17). Debate has raged about the authenticity of this passage and its significance in the argument of the epistle.[34] From a pastoral point of view, Christians have divided over its application. It certainly raises serious questions about the way in which the holiness of God's people might be compromised.

The reconciling and restoring work of God

Paul's exhortation in 2 Corinthians 6:1–12 is actually a continuation of his appeal to be reconciled to God in 5:17–20. The Corinthians were to respond appropriately to the reconciliation achieved by Christ and proclaimed by his authorized ambassadors. Rejection of Paul and his teaching would be effectively a rejection of God and his gracious offer of salvation. The sudden challenge for the church as 'the temple of the living God' to break with unbelief and idolatry (6:14 – 7:1) continues the theme of restoration and reconciliation with God.

> If God's presence really dwells among them as his temple, then they will respond and become reconciled with Paul who represents God's authoritative presence in word and Spirit' (Beale 1989: 575).[35]

More specifically, verbal links with 1 Corinthians 10:14–22 suggest that the apostle was reminding them of a particular aspect of his teaching. Under certain circumstances, he allowed his converts to eat food from the market-place that had been previously offered to the gods of paganism (1 Corinthians 8). On the other hand, he warned against the danger of actually participating in the feasts associated with idolatrous worship. As the temple of God, the church cannot associate with unbelievers 'in the temple of demons'.[36] In short, the grace of God was not to be taken as a licence for sin. Reconciliation with God meant belonging exclusively to him and being devoted to his service. Nothing must happen to hinder the renewing work of God begun among his people (*cf.* 2 Cor. 5:17).

Being mismatched with unbelievers

The strange metaphor in 2 Corinthians 6:14 recalls Deuteronomy 22:10, which forbade the yoking of an ox and ass together. Paul's meaning is, 'You must not get into double harness with unbelievers' (Barrett 1973: 195). You must not put yourself into a relationship which hinders your service to God. A series of contrasts in 6:14–16 helps to outline what this means. There can be no partnership between righteousness and lawlessness, no fellowship between light and darkness. Those who serve Christ cannot participate in the worship of Beliar (Satan). Believers cannot share with unbelievers in a way that involves the temple of God with idols.

The warning is specifically about a compromise with idolatry and it concerns the faithfulness and integrity of the church as 'the temple of the living God' (6:16). Paul supports this fundamental claim about the nature of the church with a series of Old Testament texts. The cultic regulations of the Mosaic law, which were intended to secure the holiness of God's people by isolating them from contact with the heathen, have been abolished in Christ (*cf.* Mk. 7:14–19; Acts 10:9–15; Eph. 2:14–16). Yet the separation in belief and lifestyle which those regulations sought to achieve is still required of Christians. We are not free to engage in relationships with unbelievers that jeopardize our holy fellowship with God and with one another.

The new temple expectations of the Old Testament are fulfilled in the church (*cf.* Lv. 26:12; Ezk. 37:27). We are marked off as the people of God because he dwells in our midst. The separation motif is continued in 6:17 with a quote from Isaiah 52:11 ('Therefore come out from them, and be separate from them, says the Lord, and touch nothing unclean; then I will welcome you'). This text, which originally had a cultic meaning, is related in the context to Christian belief and lifestyle. To this is attached the promise of God to be the Father of those who obey his call to holiness (cf. Ezk. 20:34, 41).

The warning of this passage must still have direct and specific application 'wherever Christians are potentially entangled in idolatry, the occult or pagan religious practices' (Barnett 1988: 131). Paul is concerned about the impact that such involvement might have on the life and witness of the local church. Can this warning also be legitimately applied to other relationships and situations? Pastorally, it has often been taken as a warning against marriages with unbelievers or business partnerships with non-Christians.

Close association with unbelievers is certainly not forbidden by Paul (cf. 1 Cor. 5:9–13; 10:27–30; 14:22–25). He actually encourages the Christian partner in a mixed marriage to maintain the relationship as long as possible and not to separate (1 Cor. 7:12–16). In such a case, the unbeliever and any offspring are described as 'consecrated' by the believing spouse (7:14, Gk. *hēgiastai*). The terminology of sanctification is clearly used in a modified sense here. Instead of defiling the believer, the unbelieving partner is brought into a relationship of special privilege and opportunity with respect to God, but is not yet converted (7:16).[37]

On the other hand, Paul does indicate that a widow is free to remarry 'only in the Lord' (1 Cor. 7:39). This suggests that Christians ought to choose partners who share their beliefs and value system. More generally, it could be said that God's people are to avoid partnerships that compromise their faith and integrity as Christians. Yet the balance of Paul's teaching about relationships with unbelievers must be carefully considered in making such a judgment.

Perfecting holiness

The promises about God dwelling in the midst of his people, and welcoming as his sons and daughters those who separate themselves from everything unclean (6:16–18), are the motivation for a holy and separated life. 'Since we have these promises', Paul says, 'let us cleanse ourselves from every defilement of body and of spirit, making holiness perfect in the fear of God' (2 Cor. 7:1). Holiness (Gk. *hagiōsynē*) is a gift bestowed on the church, resulting from God's redemptive activity and the sending of his Spirit. But the implications of this gift and status need to be worked out in everyday relationships and commitments.

Renderings such as 'perfecting holiness' (NIV) or 'making holiness perfect' (NRSV) may suggest the need for an autonomous ethical quality to be achieved by our own effort. But the Greek participle *epiteolountes* means 'discharging' or 'putting into operation', so that the challenge here is to 'keep on exercising our (quality of) sanctity (or, keep on doing the works of sanctity)' (Du Plessis 1959: 132).[38] This needs to be done 'in the fear of God', namely, with reverence and devotion to the one who is both saviour and judge of his people.

From a negative point of view, the secret of a holy life is cleansing ourselves (Gk. *katharisōmen heautous*) from 'every defilement of body and of spirit'. In terms of the exhortation in 6:17, this means deliberately separating ourselves from everything that corrupts or stains us as the holy people of God, 'outwardly and inwardly' (Barrett 1973: 202).[39]

From a positive point of view, the secret of a holy life is reflecting the character of God, knowing that his Spirit is at work amongst his people to make that separate and distinct lifestyle possible, and thus walking in the Spirit's ways. When they ignore these imperatives, believers dishonour the one who called them into an exclusive relationship with himself and compromise the holiness of the church as 'the temple of the living God' (6:16; *cf.* 1 Cor. 3:16–17; Heb. 12:15).

Progressing in godliness

In the exhortations examined so far, the emphasis has been on pursuing and expressing holiness, increasing and abounding in qualities and characteristics that are pleasing to God. At the same time, we have seen how God continues to exercise or train his people, to produce in them the signs of a transformed and sanctified life. This section considers the link between holiness and godliness, reflecting particularly on the challenges of 1 Timothy to 'train yourself in godliness' (4:7) and to pursue godliness (6:11), 'so that all may see your progress' (4:15).

Godliness in the Pastoral Epistles

Holiness terminology is rare in the Pastorals, although there is a reminder that God 'saved us and called us with a holy calling' (2 Tim. 1:9; *cf.* 1 Tim. 2:15) and the work of the Holy Spirit in regeneration and renewal is highlighted (Tit. 3:5; *cf.* 2 Tim. 1:14). Furthermore, Christians are challenged to 'cleanse themselves' from false teaching and the behaviour that flows from it (2 Tim. 2:21; *cf.* 2 Cor. 6:14 – 7:1), with the assurance that this will make them 'special utensils, dedicated [Gk. *hēgiasmenon*] and useful' to God, their rightful master. In certain respects, then, there are parallels to the teaching about holiness found elsewhere in the Pauline letters.[40]

Nevertheless, the terminology of 'godliness' or 'piety' occurs more frequently in the Pastorals than anywhere else in the New Testament and the concept is prominent in the argument.[41] The Greek noun *eusebeia* and its cognates originally denoted an attitude of piety or proper respect towards elders, masters, rulers, homeland, and the dead. When it was applied to the gods, it was used to describe conduct which accorded with the will of the gods and thus paid them the appropriate honour.[42]

Some scholars have proposed that the employment of such terminology in the Pastorals indicates the emergence of a new 'Christian citizenship ethic', more socially accommodating to the expectations and ideals of the Greco–Roman world. But Paul's use of this language is a reaction to its misapplication by false teachers in the churches. By this means he 'exhorts the Christian community to devote itself to God in every sphere of life, so that beliefs and behaviour are centred in Him' (Wainwright 1993: 223).[43] As with the theme of holiness, *separation* in values and lifestyle, rather than accommodation, is implied.

Although we cannot assume that exactly the same false teaching was being opposed in each of the Pastorals, distorted views of godliness or piety are attacked throughout. In 1 Timothy, those who do not agree with 'the sound words of our Lord Jesus Christ and the teaching that is in accordance with godliness' are described as 'conceited, understanding nothing', with 'a morbid craving for controversy and for disputes about words' (6:3–4). Such people imagine that 'godliness is a means of gain' (6:5; *cf.* Tit. 1:11). In 2 Timothy, there is warning about 'lovers of pleasure rather than lovers of God, holding to the outward form of godliness but denying its power' (3:4–5). A comparison of this passage with the denunciation of Titus 1:16 suggests that such people professed to know God, but denied him by their actions (*cf.* 1 Tim. 6:20–21).

Positively, godliness in the Pastorals appears to be the manner of life issuing from a true knowledge of God in Jesus Christ (1 Tim. 3:16; 2 Tim. 3:12; Tit. 1:1; 2:11–12). It expresses 'a spiritual devotion to God whose practice effects family and societal relationships (godly devotion)' (Wainwright 1993: 223).[44] Although the terminology of godliness has a different origin and a narrower meaning, it is used in the Pastorals as a substitute for the language of holiness in its moral or lifestyle dimension.

Training in godliness

Asceticism is repudiated in 1 Timothy 4:1–5, yet Paul urges his younger colleague to 'train' himself in godliness (4:7, Gk. *gymnaze*). Acknowledging that 'physical training is of some value' (4:8, Gk. *sōmatikē gymnasia*), the apostle is quite clear that 'godliness is valuable in every way, holding promise for both the present life and the life to come'. Athletic imagery is similarly used to encourage an appropriate form of self-discipline in 2 Timothy 2:5; 4:7 (*cf.* 1 Cor. 9:24–27). While it is true that godliness is the goal *towards* which one exercises (1 Tim. 4:7, Gk. *pros eusebeian*), the parallel with bodily exercise in the next verse suggests that we are to exercise ourselves *in* godliness (NRSV), in order to become more godly.

Since Jesus Christ is the revealed truth and power of godliness (*cf.* 1 Tim. 3:16), to exercise in godliness is 'to work out one's salvation according to the power of Christ who works within' (Knight 1992: 200; *cf.* Phil. 2:12–13). Put another way, Titus 2:11–12 asserts that 'the grace of God has appeared, bringing salvation to all, training us to renounce impiety [Gk. *asebeian*] and worldly passions, and in the present age to live lives that are self-controlled, upright, and godly [Gk. *eusebōs*]'. Here the coming of Christ is viewed as the ultimate manifestation of the grace of God. He not only provides eternal salvation but 'instructs' or 'disciplines' us (Gk. *paideuousa, cf.* Heb. 12:5–11) to renounce evil and live in a way that pleases him. The motivation for change and the power to live differently come from believing in the gospel about his grace (Tit. 2:11–14), and experiencing the regenerating and renewing work of his Spirit (3:3–7).

To 'train' oneself in godliness is to exercise the behaviour pattern demanded by the gospel. Thus, Timothy is told to exemplify what he is to teach and to be so diligent in the exercise of his ministry and the living of a godly life that all may see his 'progress' (1 Tim. 4:15, Gk. *prokopē. Cf.* Phil. 3:10–17). Elsewhere, the apostle speaks more generally about 'the progress and joy in faith' of believers (Phil. 1:25). Such texts expect change and development in God's people, resulting from his gracious work in them, enabling them to do his will.

Conclusion

The challenges to holiness examined in this chapter convey both warning and encouragement. No Christian should doubt the need to give practical, everyday expression to the holiness that is our status and calling in Christ. Only those who trust in his sanctifying work on the cross, and take seriously the warning to 'pursue holiness', will 'see the Lord'. The message that God is pleased by holiness and outraged by unholiness particularly needs to be heard by a generation that focuses on 'fun and fulfillment, ego-massage and techniques for present success, and public issues that carry no challenge to one's personal morals' (Packer 1992: 9).

On the other hand, it is possible to be so zealous for 'progress' that one's attention shifts from God's grace to human effort. Moral growth and development will be God's gift to us at different stages of our lives, but spirituality must not be measured in terms of the rate of change. We are to go on exhibiting what we know of God's character and will, motivated by the certainty of his acceptance, cleansing and enabling in Christ, together with the promise of entire sanctification when we meet him, face to face. Progress may be seen as we exercise ourselves in that godly devotion which issues from a true knowledge of God in Jesus Christ.

These gospel perspectives on the Christian life must not be obscured by the uncertainty of a moralistic perfectionism. Scripture emphasizes that holiness is a divine gift – a share in the life and character of God. In practical, everyday terms it means being dedicated to God and separated from all that is sinful. This condition needs to be renewed and re-expressed every day, especially when testing comes or fresh challenges to please God confront us.

> The progress of sanctification, therefore, is a process comparable with no other process. Too often analogies and metaphors have done violence to its unique character. For progress in sanctification never meant working out one's own salvation under one's own auspices; on the contrary, it meant working out one's own salvation with a rising sense of dependence on God's grace (Berkouwer 1952: 112).

Chapter Five

Living between the cross and the resurrection

John Calvin (1509–64) was the first of the Reformers to make a distinction between the concepts of justification and sanctification. Like Luther before him, he insisted that justification is simply the declaration of God that we are righteous because of the righteousness of Christ. Like Luther, he also stressed the personal union of the believer with Christ as the key to salvation. For Calvin, however, justification and sanctification were two distinct but inseparable consequences of incorporation into Christ: 'Christ justifies no one whom he does not at the same time sanctify. These benefits are joined together by an everlasting and indissoluble bond' (*Inst.* 3.16.1).[1]

Calvin identified the Holy Spirit as 'the bond by which Christ effectually unites us to himself' (*Inst.* 3.1.1.).[2] Faith in Christ is the principal work of the Spirit, sustaining and strengthening the godly to persevere in the face of every temptation and trial. Faith is the key to a sanctified life. Calvin develops what I have called a definitive or positional view of sanctification but goes on to talk about the outworking of sanctification in the life of the believer. God consecrates us to himself 'as temples', as he wipes out our corruptions and cleanses us from guilt. The Spirit, who brings us 'purged of uncleanness and defilement into obedience to God's righteousness', then begins to impart to us some of the actual holiness which dwelt in Christ (*Inst.* 3.3.14).[3]

When he moves to consider how justification by faith can lead to holiness of life, Calvin emphasizes the role of *repentance*. Repentance not only follows faith but is born of faith. Repentance means 'the true turning of our life to God, a turning that arises from a pure and honest fear of him' (*Inst.* 3.3.5).[4] It consists in 'mortification of our flesh and of the old man' and in 'vivification of the Spirit'. Mortification means putting off the old self, renouncing the world, the flesh and evil desires.

Vivification means being renewed in Christ. Both things happen to us by participation in Christ.

Calvin therefore interprets repentance as *our* part in a divine process which he calls 'regeneration'. The sole end of this process is 'to restore in us the image of God that had been disfigured and all but obliterated through Adam's transgression' (*Inst.* 3.3.9).[5] Thus, he uses the language of repentance and regeneration to outline the way sanctification proceeds from our union with Christ. Sanctification is not only a gift to be received but a life to be lived, as we yield up ourselves 'to be conformed to Jesus Christ in his death and resurrection, renouncing the world and all our sins' (Wallace 1959: 28).

Diagrammatically, Calvin's approach can be represented like this:

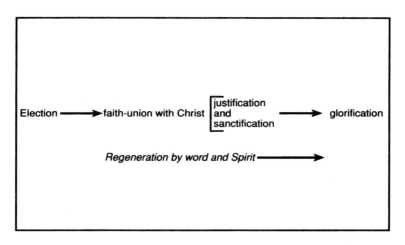

In many respects, this teaching was foundational for subsequent debates about sanctification. Even when they did not agree with his conclusions, many took Calvin's insights as the starting-point for the development of their own theories. Calvin was particularly concerned to give an appropriate description of what happens between the beginning of the Christian life and its end in glory. As an astute interpreter of Paul, he sought to relate the doctrine of sanctification to the apostle's eschatology. In other words, he took seriously the tension between the 'now' and the 'not yet' in New Testament teaching and applied it to the subject of holiness.

In this chapter, I want to explore the idea that moral renewal proceeds from our union with Christ in his death and resurrection. How does this happen? What part do we play and what is the role of the Holy Spirit? What change can we legitimately expect in this life, given the ongoing power of sin and the flesh? I will begin to answer these questions, as Calvin and many others have done, by focusing on Paul's argument in Romans 6 – 8. In chapter six, I extend the investigation to other Pauline passages.

Romans 6 – 8 in context

Although the terminology of sanctification is found only in 6:19 and 22, these chapters have often been characterized as a classic statement of the doctrine. An overview of their argument will follow, taking special note of parallels with the teaching about sanctification uncovered elsewhere in Paul's writings. But first it is important to note the flow of the preceding chapters.

The theme of Romans 1 – 4 is the revelation of God's righteousness or covenant faithfulness (1:16–17; 3:1–6, 21–22).[6] This has now been disclosed through the gospel, 'apart from the law', for the benefit all who believe, Jews and Gentiles alike. God's righteousness is paradoxically revealed by his willingness to justify or declare righteous all who have sinned and fall short of the glory of God (1:23–24)![7] Such acquittal is made possible 'by his grace as a gift, through the redemption that is in Christ Jesus, whom God put forward as a sacrifice of atonement by his blood, effective through faith' (1:24–25).

Paul's gospel of justification by faith rules out the possibility of putting any confidence in 'works prescribed by the law' (3:28, Gk. *ergōn nomou*).[8] Jew and Gentile can now be justified on the same basis, without God's law being overthrown (3:29–31). Indeed, Romans 4 shows how the original covenant promises to Abraham have been fulfilled in Jesus Christ. Abraham is the father of *all* who believe and have righteousness reckoned to them by God.

Romans 5 is a bridge passage, providing a powerful conclusion to this first major section of the argument and preparing for what follows.[9] The apostle begins to concentrate on the outworking of the gospel in relation to the individual. At the same time, he highlights the already / not-yet tension, which is part of our present experience as Christians (5:1–11).

The whole sweep of human history is then embraced in a comparison between Adam and Christ (5:12–21). Sin and death are presented as powers that rule the offspring of Adam. By his disobedience, Adam determined the character and outcome of the present evil age. By his obedience, however, Christ has determined the character and outcome of a new age. Those who 'receive the abundance of grace and the free gift of righteousness' from Jesus Christ belong to that new age and 'rule in life with him' (5:17; cf. 5:21).

This concept of the two ages is the basis of Paul's teaching in Romans 6 – 8. Those who belong to the new age are liberated through Christ, but are not yet entirely free from the old age. We suffer from living in the overlap of the ages. With this in mind, Paul seeks to clarify the extent to which sin, death, law and flesh continue to affect the lives of those who are justified by faith.[10]

The Christian and sin in Romans 6

In Romans 6:1–11, the apostle speaks in absolute terms about the way sin and death lose their hold on those ruled by God's grace in Jesus Christ. The exhortation in 6:12–23, however, indicates that we are still vulnerable to the claim of those powers. We must make choices that are consistent with our new standing in Christ.

Dead to sin and alive to God

Paul's opening question, 'Should we continue in sin in order that grace may abound?' (6:1), forestalls a wrong inference from 5:20. There he argued that grace abounded where sin increased. So does it follow that the more we sin, the more God's grace will be seen? Such objections were doubtless voiced by Paul's opponents from time to time (cf. 3:7–8), but it is likely that he posed the question himself here, to advance the argument. Put another way, the charge could be made that his law-free gospel brings no obligation to seek righteousness of life.

An emphatic denial quickly dismisses such logic ('By no means!'). With a second question, Paul effectively answers the problem he has raised, 'How can we who died to sin go on living in it?' (6:2). For the first time in this letter, the language of death is used to describe *the situation of the Christian.* But how can we be 'dead to sin'? Has sin lost its power? What sort of change does Paul envisage taking place in us? The passage that follows suggests four different, but closely related, senses in which Christians die to sin.

Fundamentally, there is the *judicial* sense. Christians died to sin in God's sight when Christ died on the cross for them. God's decision 'to take their sins upon himself in the person of his dear Son may be said to be tantamount to a decision to see them as having died in Christ's death' (Cranfield 1975: 299; *cf.* 2 Cor. 5:14).[11] This sense is particularly brought out by the expression, 'our old self was crucified with him' in 6:6 (*cf.* Gal. 2:19; 6:14). Our human condition in Adam (Gk. *ho palaios hēmōn anthrōpos*), dominated by sin and death (5:12–21), was literally 'crucified together with' Christ on his cross (Gk. *synestaurōthē*). Paul is not talking here about a change in our natures, the replacement of an 'old nature' with a 'new nature'. The reference is to Christians corporately, for whom the rule of sin has been broken by Christ in his death.[12] Individually it may be said that, 'what was crucified with Christ was not a part of me called my old nature, but the whole of me as I was before I was converted' (Stott 1966: 45).[13]

At one level, Romans 6:2–11 is a restatement of the doctrine of justification by faith. At another level, it is a statement of eschatology. When Christ died to sin, it was the end of one epoch in human history and the beginning of another. Believers have died to sin inasmuch as they have been transferred from the old epoch to the new.[14] In other words, Paul's thought in Romans 6 is still very much determined by the Adam / Christ contrast in Romans 5.

The second sense in which Christians have died to sin may be called *baptismal*. The apostle goes on to remind his readers that 'all of us who have been baptized into Christ Jesus were baptized into his death' (6:3). Baptism into union with Christ is the way we identify with him in his epoch-changing death and draw on its benefits. Of course, conversion and water baptism are often separated in Christian experience. But Paul's point is that genuine initiation into Christ means trusting in his death as our death and his risen life as our life. In this respect, baptism is presented as our 'funeral rite' and a decisive break with the life and values of this present age.[15]

The third sense in which Christians die to sin is *moral*. This emerges with the second reference to baptism in 6:4. 'Therefore we have been buried with him by baptism into death, so that, just as Christ was raised from the dead by the glory of the Father, so we too might walk in newness of life.' The outworking of Christ's death and resurrection for us now is not yet sinlessness or bodily resurrection. Paul's purpose clause (Gk. *hina . . . peripatēsōmen*, 'so that we might walk') indicates God's *intention* for us but does not promise perfection in this life. As we await the consummation of God's purposes, we are called to live as those who belong to the risen Lord Jesus. So the point of his death and resurrection and our union with him was not that we should 'continue in sin' (6:1) but rather 'walk in newness of life' (6:4).

The fourth sense in which Christians die to sin is *literal*. Those who have been united with him in a death like his, will actually be united with him in a resurrection like his (6:5).[16] Just as Christ, being raised from the dead, 'will never die again; death no longer has dominion over him' (6:9), so Christians will experience resurrection from death and complete liberation from the power and effect of sin. We are to live in the present as those expecting to share the ultimate renewal of all things with him. Even though we have yet to participate in that resurrection, 'its power already rules us and sets us in the new walk' (Käsemann 1980: 169).

Paul's 'inaugurated eschatology' is revealed in the way he parallels Christ's death and resurrection with our own:

Christ died and was buried	We were baptized into his death (6:3) and buried with him in baptism (6:4)
Christ was raised from the dead	So that we could now walk in newness of life (6:4) *and* Ultimately be united with him in a resurrection like his (6:5)

Freedom from sin?

Paul has sometimes been taken to mean that complete freedom from sin should be our present experience. Our old self was crucified with Christ, he declares, 'so that the body of sin might be destroyed, and we might no longer be enslaved to sin' (6:6). Is this a promise of absolute deliverance from sin's power? 'The body of sin' appears to be a way of speaking about the whole person as controlled by sin. Our sinful self was hanged on the cross with Christ so that 'the body as a helpless tool of sin might be definitively defeated' (Moo 1991:393).[17] As in 6:4, however, a purpose clause indicates God's intention in a timeless and summary way (Gk. *hina katargēthē*, 'so that [the body of sin] might be destroyed'). Paul calls us to live in the light of God's ultimate goal for us.

The eschatological tension in Paul's thinking needs to be recalled here. Our rescue from the dominion of sin will only be complete when we are physically resurrected and transformed. Yet, even now, God's purpose is that 'we might no longer be enslaved to sin' (6:6).[18] The way in which that liberty is to be experienced is set out in 6:11–14.

Meanwhile, the apostle illustrates his point by reference to a general truth, 'for whoever has died is freed from sin' (6:7, Gk. *dedikaiōtai apo tēs hamartias*). He means that dead people are no longer answerable for sin.[19] But there is a deliberate play on words here. The fact that God has 'justified' us (Gk. *dedikaiōtai*) is the basis of a new freedom to live as those who have 'died to sin', with the possibility of resisting sin in our lives.

Those who have 'died with Christ' will also live with him in that state beyond death, where 'death no longer has dominion over him' (6:8–9). As a man, Jesus was subject to the power of sin and death, even though he never succumbed to sin. When he died, 'he died to sin once for all', so that he now 'lives to God', entirely unencumbered by sin and death (6:10). These verses emphasize that freedom from sin in an absolute sense is only possible for those who share in Christ's bodily resurrection. Nevertheless, his resurrection life casts its shadow into the present, and gives us the promise of defeating sin and living for God here and now.

The point of the argument in 6:6–10 is that *the hope of physical resurrection* is as much an empowerment for godly living as the certainty that, *on the cross, sin's penalty was paid*. Those who belong to the crucified and resurrected Lord Jesus need no longer live as the helpless slaves of sin.

Living it out

Romans 6:2–10 expresses in different language the definitive view of sanctification found elsewhere in Paul's letters (*e.g.* 1 Cor. 6:11; Eph. 5:25–26; 2 Thes. 2:13–14). God has consecrated to himself a new people, through the death and resurrection of his Son. By faith, we have been buried together with him by baptism into death, united with him in a death like his. God has dealt with our sins and bound us to himself, making it possible for us to live a new life to his glory and ultimately to be united with Christ in a resurrection like his.

The challenge, then, is for us to live out and experience the benefits of God's sanctifying work in Christ. Paul first puts it this way: 'So you also must consider yourselves dead to sin and alive to God in Christ Jesus' (6:11). The imperative 'consider' (Gk. *logizesthe*) does not mean 'pretend' but, in effect, 'recognize what the truth of the gospel means'.[20] We are to go on viewing ourselves as God does, when he refuses to 'reckon' sin against us and reckons righteousness to us, apart from works (*cf.* 4:5–8). He regards us as being 'dead to sin and alive to God in Christ Jesus'. We should regard ourselves in the same way!

Two negative exhortations and a positive one follow. Paul's first challenge is, 'Therefore, do not let sin exercise dominion in your mortal bodies, to make you obey their passions' (6:12). Christians must not let sin 'go on reigning unopposed over their daily life' (Cranfield 1975: 316),[21] but must revolt in the name of God, their rightful ruler. If they fail to respond to this challenge, they will be driven further and further in obedience to the passions or lusts of their fallen nature. Use of the word 'passions' here is significant (Gk. *tais epithymiais*). It denotes physical and emotional needs which can overwhelm believers and usurp God's rule in their lives unless checked (*cf.* Rom. 13:14; Gal. 5:16–17; Col. 3:5).

So Paul's second warning is, 'No longer present your members to sin as instruments of wickedness [unrighteousness]' (6:13a; *cf.* 7:23). The way to resist sin is to stop placing ourselves and our capacities at sin's disposal. Attached to this warning is the positive alternative that makes resistance to sin possible. 'Present yourselves to God as those who have been brought from death to life, and present your members to God as instruments of righteousness' (6:13b; *cf.* 12:1). We have a profound obligation to the one who has brought us 'from death to life'. Christ's death and resurrection have made possible a profound change of attitude and motivation, a real sense of belonging to him, and a new freedom to resist sin and serve God because of justification.

Righteousness and unrighteousness are contrasted in 6:13 as powers that can control the human personality. Indeed, in 6:18–20, being a slave of righteousness is another way of speaking about being enslaved to God. So righteousness is not something under our control, which we can 'do' to please God. It is not simply a moral standard for us to follow. Righteousness is the manner and mode in which God manifests himself, supremely in justifying sinners who trust in Christ. It is 'the gracious power of God which claims and sustains the believer and reaches its final expression in eternal life (5:21; 6:23)' (Dunn 1988a: 335).[22]

'Grace' is similarly used in 6:14 to describe the way God rules over us in Christ. 'Sin will have no dominion over you,' the apostle insists, 'since you are not under law but under grace.' Sin will not be lord of those who have been captured by God's grace through the gospel. The precise link between sin and the law remains to be explained in Romans 7. The power for change comes with the knowledge that we are not under the law's condemnation, nor even under the law as a system of relating to God. We are simply ruled by his grace in Christ Jesus.[23]

Choosing your master

Anticipating a misinterpretation of what he has just said, Paul poses another question. 'What then? Should we sin because we are not under law but under grace?' (6:15). He quickly puts paid to this suggestion that those under grace are free to sin. Whatever is the power to which you willingly yield yourselves, he insists, you are *slaves* of the power you obey, and you only have two powers from which to choose (6:16).

A series of antitheses then highlight the contrast between the two dominions and their effect:

Slavery to sin leads to death	Slavery to obedience leads to righteousness ·
Slavery to impurity and to lawlessness results in lawlessness	Slavery to righteousness results in holiness
Slavery to sin means being free in regard to righteousness	Freedom from sin means being enslaved to God, with holiness as the fruit and eternal life as the end
The wages of sin is death	But the free gift of God is eternal life

People show by their conduct whose slaves they are and what their destiny is. Enslavement to sin leads to lawlessness and ultimately death. Enslavement to righteousness, which is another way of speaking about enslavement to God, leads to holiness and ultimately eternal life. True freedom can only be found in the service of God.

A key verse has been omitted from this chart: 'But thanks be to God that you, having once been slaves of sin, have become obedient from the heart to the form of teaching to which you were entrusted' (6:17). Paul's readers moved from one category of slavery to another when they responded to the gospel about God's righteousness and grace. They became obedient 'from the heart', signifying a commitment deeply rooted in their innermost being (cf. 2:15, 29; 5:5; 10:9–10). This is another way of expressing the sanctifying work of God through the gospel and the operation of his Spirit.

The master to whose control Christians have been transferred is here strangely described as 'a form of teaching' (Gk. *typon didachēs*). Paul is thinking about the gospel of Christ as 'a mould which gives to the new life its appropriate shape or pattern' (Beare 1958–59: 210). Clearly, at the heart of this is Christ himself, who is the pattern for Christian living (cf. Col. 2:6). But it is also possible that fundamental ethical principles were included in the 'form of teaching' that Paul had in mind.

When we transfer from the service of sin to the service of righteousness, we are freed from the old master and bound to the new one (6:18). Paul apologizes for the inadequacy of his language but has used the harsh and rather humiliating imagery of slavery to make a point that his readers may have overlooked. They once yielded their 'members' as 'slaves to impurity and lawlessness' and the resulting state or condition was lawlessness (6:19a, Gk. *eis tēn anomian*).[24] Now they are to present themselves as slaves of righteousness and the resulting state or condition will be holiness (6:19b, Gk. *eis hagiasmon*). Put another way, the 'fruit' of submission to God is holiness (6:22; *cf.* 1 Tim. 2:15) and the 'end' or 'goal' is eternal life.

I have opted for 'holiness' as the translation of *hagiasmos* in 6:19 and 22, because the earlier part of Romans 6 presents a definitive view of sanctification through the death of Christ. What flows from this is holiness or sanctification as a state or condition that needs to be expressed in everyday life. It is possible that sanctification as a process of moral renewal could be understood in this context,[25] though this is less likely in view of Paul's use of this term elsewhere. 'Holiness' or 'sanctification' is the alternative to the *condition* of uncleanness and lawlessness from which we were rescued.

As noted elsewhere, the moral aspect of sanctification is secondary to its 'soteriological' reference (*cf.* 1 Cor. 1:30; 1 Thes. 4: 3, 4, 7; 2 Thes. 2:13; Heb. 12:14; 1 Pet. 1:2). Sanctification in the New Testament 'consists not in a particular moral quality which has been attained, but in a particular relationship to God which has been given' (Furnish 1968: 155).[26] This is in keeping with the soteriological and cultic use of the terminology in the Old Testament. The ethical demand of sanctification arises out of the saving activity by which God consecrates us to himself as a distinct and dedicated people.

The Christian and God's law in Romans 7

Paul's presentation of the gospel in Romans never moves far away from the question of God's law and its role in his saving plan (*cf.* 3:19–20, 21, 27–28; 4:13–15; 5:13–14, 20; 6:14). In Romans 7, the issue is finally addressed in some detail. Vigorous debates continue to take place about the identification of the person depicted in 7:7–25. Is it Paul the Christian or Israel under the law? Is it unregenerate humanity or the backsliding Christian? Such views are clearly linked to different theologies of sanctification.

Anthropology, however, is a subordinate issue in this chapter, where the main topic is the Mosaic law. The apostle first argues that bondage to the law must cease if anyone is to be joined to Christ (7:1–6). He then shows that, although the law is 'holy and just and good', it has become 'the unwitting tool of sin, being used to confirm and imprison in death' (Moo 1991: 433; 7:7–25). Despite its divine origin, the law as a written code can neither justify nor sanctify, because of the ongoing power of sin.

Belonging to Christ

The chapter begins by enunciating a basic principle, 'that the law is binding on a person only during that person's lifetime' (7:1). Paul illustrates this with reference to marriage. When a husband dies, his wife is discharged 'from the law concerning the husband' and she is free to marry another (7:2–3). The principle is then applied to Paul's readers. 'In the same way, my friends, you have died to the law through the body of Christ, so that you may belong to another, to him who has been raised from the dead in order that we may bear fruit for God' (7:4). In the illustration, only the husband dies, but in the application, Christians die with Christ.

Paul makes several points about the law here that were made about sin in Romans 6. As we 'died to sin' by being baptized into Christ's death (6:2–3), so we 'died to the law through the body of Christ' (7:4).[27] Christians have been delivered by Christ's death from the condemnation of the law (cf. 8:1) and also from its mastery or rule (cf. 7:1). Like sin, the law is viewed as a power of the old era, from which we need to be 'discharged' (7:6, Gk. *katērgthēmen. Cf.* 6:6, 14; 7:2). The believer is transferred from the old era to the new by identifying with Christ in his death.

In this matter, Paul is more radical than many of his interpreters. Death to the law has the purpose of setting us free from the law so that we may be 'wedded' to Christ (7:4, echoing the language of 7:3). The view that we are not under the law as a means of salvation but remain under it as a rule of life is not a distinction that Paul makes. In his own experience, 'allegiance to a person had displaced devotion to a code – which was, indeed, not merely a code but more a way of life' (Bruce 1977: 189).[28] Romans 7 makes it clear that such a transfer of allegiance is the logical consequence for all who trust in Christ's atoning death. The purpose of this liberation from the law and union with Christ is that 'we may bear fruit for God' (7:4; *cf.* 6:18–22).

But why is the issue so black and white?

> While we were living in the flesh, our sinful passions, aroused by the law, were at work in our members to bear fruit for death. But now we are discharged from the law, dead to that which held us captive, so that we are slaves not under the old written code but in the new life of the Spirit (7:5–6).

These verses introduce the main emphases of chapters 7 – 8.

Pre-Christian existence is depicted as being 'in the flesh' (7:5, Gk. *en tē sarki*), which means more than being 'controlled by the sinful nature' (NIV). Being 'in the flesh' means, more broadly, being dominated and controlled by 'this-worldly principles and values' (Moo 1991: 442),[29] as well as by the demands of self. According to Romans 8:9, this is a situation from which one is delivered by belonging to Christ and being given his Spirit.

Existence in the domain of flesh is controlled by the three great powers of the old era, sin, the law and death. In an astonishing statement that begs for further explanation, Paul declares that 'our sinful passions *aroused by the law*' were actually operative in our faculties to produce behaviour worthy of God's judgment (7:5). The law had a greenhouse effect, 'forcing the growth of sin to bring forth the fruit of death' (Dunn 1988a: 371–372). When we turned to Christ, however, we were 'discharged from the law', having died to 'that which held us captive', so that we might serve God, literally, 'in newness of Spirit and not in oldness of letter' (7:6).

This letter / Spirit contrast is another way of highlighting the difference between the old era and the new, the one characterized by law and the other by Spirit (*cf.* 2:27–9; 2 Cor. 3:6–9, 14). Under the New Covenant, the sanctified life is ruled by Christ through his Spirit, not by the law (*cf.* my Appendix B). Paul does not elaborate on this new life in the Spirit until he reaches Romans 8, though there are anticipations of his argument later in Romans 7.

The law and sin

Paul's treatment of the law has so closely linked it with sin that he recognizes the possibility of inferring that 'the law is sin' (7:7). Emphatically denying this, he responds with a positive statement about the role of the law. 'If it had not been for the law, I would not have known sin. I would not have known what it is to covet if the law had not said, "You shall not covet." ' Of course people sin where there is no law (*cf.* 5:13), but they do not recognize it for what it is until faced with an explicit command of God (*cf.* 3:20)

The apostle does not simply speak about his own experience in 7:7–11. He uses the first person singular to speak representatively, though in a way that emphasizes his own involvement in the situation (*cf.* 3:7). Most obviously, he refers to the experience of Israel, as the people uniquely privileged to receive the law of God. There are also allusions to the story of Adam, who was 'alive' before the commandment came (*cf.* Gn. 2:17), but who 'died' when sin sprang to life (*cf.* Gn. 3:17–19). The point is that, when the Israelites received God's law, they repeated Adam's sin and found themselves to be under God's judgment. This was so 'because of their participation in Adamic humanity' (Wright 1991: 195).[30]

Humanity's story is dramatized and concentrated in the history of Israel. The real culprit, however, is not law but *sin*, 'seizing an opportunity in the commandment' (7:8, 11). What was true in Eden and at Sinai is also true in everyday experience. Sin takes advantage of the law, perverting its function, so that the commandment designed to expose and check covetousness actually produces in me 'all kinds of covetousness'. Were it not for sin, the commandment would have promoted life, but because of sin, the commandment promotes death (7:9–10). Sin's blatant misuse of God's holy law reveals its true character as 'a dynamic overlord that induces a spirit of rebellion against God and of disobedience to his commandments' (Fitzmyer 1992: 463; Rom. 7:12–13).

Flesh, law and Spirit

In the concluding verses of Romans 7, Paul continues to expose the inability of the law to bring about holiness and righteousness. In so doing, he introduces a note of eschatological tension familiar to us from the end of chapter 6. Having stressed the discontinuity of the old and the new age in 7:1–6, he points to the continuity or *overlap* of the ages in 7:14–25. 'We know that the law is spiritual', he says (7:14a), suggesting that the law cannot be 'consigned without remainder to the old epoch of Adam' (Dunn 1988a: 406).[31] In a sense, the law belongs to both epochs (*cf.* Appendix B), but so do 'I', because 'I am of the flesh, sold into slavery under sin' (7:14b)!

Although Paul continues to use the first person singular here, he shifts from the past tense to the present. He speaks as one who is still in the realm of the flesh (Gk. *sarkinos*), living in the epoch which is ruled by sin and death. With this 'I' (Gk. *egō*) he includes other believers, who belong to Christ and his epoch but are still part of Adam and his epoch.

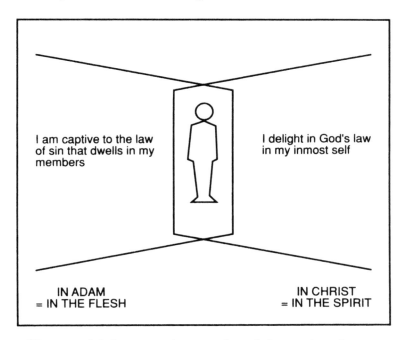

I am captive to the law of sin that dwells in my members

I delight in God's law in my inmost self

IN ADAM
= IN THE FLESH

IN CHRIST
= IN THE SPIRIT

The apostle's language is so stark and depressing that many have considered him to be speaking as a representative of unregenerate humanity, or as a Jew living under the law of Moses.[32] Others have suggested that he describes a stage of the Christian life which can be left behind.[33] But Paul's desire to keep the law of God is hardly the confession of an unregenerate person (*cf.* 8:7) and his anguish over failure is hardly consistent with that self-righteousness he betrayed as a Pharisee (*cf.* Phil. 3:4–6). The struggle that Romans 7 portrays cannot be divorced from the picture of conflict in the Christian life set forth in 6:12–23 (*cf.* Gal. 5:16–26).[34]

There is clearly a difference between the condition described in 7:14 and the unregenerate life 'in the flesh' mentioned in 7:5 and 8:5–8. The Christian does not any longer live a life fundamentally determined and controlled by the flesh. Nevertheless, 'flesh' continues to be a powerful force in our experience. The conflict with sin does not diminish with conversion but actually intensifies, because we begin to experience the possibilities of a Spirit-directed life (*cf.* Gal. 5:16–26).

In 7:15–20, Paul speaks as one who struggles with sin while seeking to serve God 'in the new life of the Spirit' (7:6). What he does as one 'sold under sin' he hates. What he desires to do as a servant of God he does not always accomplish. Even though he paints the 'I' in blackest terms (7:14), there is also a sense in which 'I' can stand back and honestly say, 'it is no longer I that do it, but sin that dwells within me' (7:20; *cf.* 7:17). The split is not between 'I' and the flesh but between 'I' as one inextricably bound up with the flesh and 'I' as someone belonging to Christ and the age to come.[35]

Returning specifically to the subject of the law, Paul indicates the way he finds the law to operate with respect to himself: 'when I want to do what is good, evil lies close at hand' (7:21). He continues, 'I delight in the law of God in my inmost self, but I see in my members another law at war with the law of my mind, making me captive to the law of sin that dwells in my members' (7:22–23). The 'inmost self' (Gk. *ton esō anthrōpon*) is the aspect of Paul which he describes as being 'renewed day by day' in 2 Corinthians 4:16 (*cf.* Eph. 3:16). Romans 7:22 appears to be speaking about the way God enables the people of the New Covenant to have a proper appreciation of his law and the desire to obey him from the heart.[36] A parallel expression in 7:25 ('with my mind I am a slave to the law of God') suggests that the renewal of the mind is fundamental to this commitment (*cf.* 12:2).

When Paul refers to 'the law of sin' (7:23, 25), it is possible that he is speaking metaphorically of 'the power of sin'. It is also possible that he is using the word 'law' consistently throughout the chapter to describe the law of Moses. On this reading, 'the law of sin' means 'the law used by sin to deceive and kill' (*cf.* 7:11).[37] In other words, there are two different ways of viewing and relating to the law of God. 'The law of my mind' is the law which my renewed mind acknowledges as the good and perfect will of God. 'The law of sin' is the law as used by sin to deceive and kill.[38]

Paul reverts to the idea that the law is a power dominating the Adamic era (5:20–21; 6:14) and mentions 'another law at war with the law of my mind, making me captive to the law of sin that dwells in my members' (7:23). The law is at work 'in my members' because there the law is sin's instrument. Military metaphors are used to describe a conflict in which victory regularly goes to 'the law of sin' (7:23). In other words, even the law acknowledged as 'holy' and 'spiritual' is not strong enough to defeat the power of sin. 'When the options are analysed solely in terms of sin and the law, defeat is invariable, for the law is no match for sin' (Dunn 1988a: 410).[39]

'Wretched man that I am! Who will rescue me from this body of death?' (7:24), is not a cry of despair but a cry of frustration and longing. It is the groaning of the Spirit-led person for the fullness of redemption that will take place when our bodies are resurrected (*cf.* 8:11, 23).[40] Only then will we be free from endless warfare with sin, death, flesh and the law. So Paul's thanksgiving in 7:25a ('Thanks be to God through Jesus Christ our Lord!') is an expression of confidence in God and the outworking of his saving plan.

Meanwhile, he returns to the note of conflict that has marked 7:14–23. 'So then, with my mind I am a slave to the law of God, but with my flesh I am a slave to the law of sin' (7:25b). Serving the law of God 'with my mind' means serving God as one who is being renewed by the Spirit of God. At the same time, flesh perverts the law to make it 'the law of sin'. Moreover, serving 'the law of sin' with my flesh means continuing to misuse the law and to resist God's will.

The Christian and God's Spirit in Romans 8

The declaration that there is 'therefore now no condemnation for those who are in Christ Jesus' (8:1) recalls the end of

Romans 5. There Paul asserts that Adam's sin brought condemnation for all, whereas Christ's act of righteousness leads to 'justification and life for all' (5:16, 18). The divine condemnation for sin, expressed through the law of God, has been experienced by Christ in his death, thus discharging those who are in Christ from that condemnation (8:1, 3; *cf.* 5:1).

Paul's 'therefore now' in 8:1 also recalls 7:6, that '*now* we are discharged from the law, dead to that which held us captive'.[41] Chapter 8 begins, as chapters 6 and 7 began, with a statement of what Christ has already accomplished for us. On this basis, Paul shows how the Spirit can enable those who are still part of old age to live as those who belong to the new age, serving God 'in the new life of the Spirit' (7:6). Reaffirming the idea that new life flows from the justifying work of Christ, he takes the opportunity to enlarge on the ministry of the Holy Spirit, only briefly mentioned in 5:5 and 7:6.

Fulfilment of the law in Christ

Paul significantly advances the argument of these chapters when he introduces the Holy Spirit as 'a key agent of liberation from the old realm of sin and death' (Moo 1991: 509):[42] 'for the law of the Spirit of life in Christ Jesus has set you free from the law of sin and death' (8:2). If the word 'law' is used consistently in these chapters, 'the law of sin and death' will mean the law caught up in the nexus of sin and death (*cf.* 7:23, 25) and 'the law of the Spirit of life in Christ Jesus' will mean the law *as fulfilled in Christ through the Spirit*.[43] On the other hand, if the apostle is engaging in a word play, identifying the Spirit as another 'law', his point will be that the Spirit is 'the divine antidote to the two former "laws" (sin *and* Torah)' (Fee 1994: 522).

The liberation mentioned in 8:2, like the liberation from sin proclaimed in 6:18 and 22, was effected 'in Christ Jesus'. The benefits of that liberation are applied to believers by the indwelling Spirit. 'The law weakened by the flesh' could not achieve liberation from sin or bring eternal life (8:3). Only the obedience and death of the Son of God could free us from the law's condemnation. He fulfilled the law perfectly and yet sin was condemned *in his flesh*.

God's intention, however, was not simply to release us from condemnation in Christ. It was to make it possible for 'the just requirement of the law' to be fulfilled in us, 'who walk not according to the flesh but according to the Spirit' (8:4). The expression 'the just requirement of the law' (Gk. *to dikaiōma tou nomou*) points to the law's essential requirement.[44] The gift of the Spirit to those who are justified by faith in Christ brings about the obedience from the heart which the law demanded (*cf.* Dt. 6:4–5; Lv. 19:18; Rom. 2:28–29), fulfilling the promise of the New Covenant (*cf.* Je. 31:31–34; Ezk. 36:25–27). It is the obedience which proceeds from faith.

Paul does not envisage a sinless life here or one removed from the temptation and struggle portrayed in Romans 6 – 7. Indeed, he does not say that *we* fulfil what the law requires but that its just requirement 'might be fulfilled in us' (Gk. *plērōthē*), the passive signalling the activity of God's Spirit. The law's require-ment is fulfilled 'in us' when we are enabled to live under the direction and control of the Holy Spirit.

> God not only provides in Christ the full completion of the law's demands for the believer, he also sends the Spirit into his or her heart to empower a new obedience to his demands' (Moo 1991: 517).[45]

The Spirit of life

The unbreakable link between Spirit and life on the one hand and flesh and death on the other is maintained in 8:5–13. Living according to the flesh means setting your mind on the things of the flesh, whereas living according to the Spirit means setting your mind on the things of the Spirit.

> It is a question of our preoccupations, the ambitions which compel us and the interests which engross us; how we spend our time, money and energy; what we give ourselves up to (Stott 1966: 87).

The results of these two different 'minds' are death on the one hand and life and peace on the other (8:6). The 'mind of the flesh' must have death as its fruit because it is fundamentally hostile to God and will not submit to his law – 'indeed it cannot' (8:7–8).

Paul sharply contrasts those who are in the flesh (the unregenerate) and those who are in the Spirit (the regenerate), making it clear that those who have been justified by faith are indwelt by the Spirit of God and are, by God's grace, already 'in the Spirit' (8:9). Those who lack the Spirit lack the life and liberation that the Spirit brings (8:10–11). This prepares for the challenge of 8:12–13, warning Christians about the danger of living as if they were still in the flesh.[46]

By the Spirit, Christ himself dwells in those who belong to him (8:10, cf. 'the Spirit of Christ' in 8:9). This indwelling brings new life in the present, even though our mortal bodies continue to move towards physical death because of sin. The message of the first segment of Romans 8 is brought to a fitting climax with the declaration that 'the Spirit is *life* because of righteousness' or 'because of justification' (8:10, Gk. *dia dikaiosynē*). Furthermore, the indwelling Spirit is the pledge of ultimate victory in bodily resurrection with Christ (8:11, cf. 8:23, 'the redemption of our bodies').

Living it out

As in Romans 6:11–14, an exhortation now flows directly out of the presentation of God's saving work in the first part of the chapter. Those who are indwelt by the Holy Spirit are 'debtors, not to the flesh, to live according to the flesh', but (presumably Paul intended to say) debtors to the Spirit to live according to the Spirit (8:12). Yielding to the flesh is certainly no impossibility, but we have a new obligation to holiness impressed upon us by the Spirit.

Once again the apostle asserts that the outcome of living 'according to the flesh' is death without any hope of resurrection to life with Christ (8:13). However, if by the Spirit's direction and power we go on putting to death (Gk. *thanatoute*) 'the deeds of the body', meaning a ruthless rejection of all those practices we know to be sinful, we will live.[47] Although the focus here is on 'deeds' carried out under the influence of the flesh, the context makes it clear that Paul is also calling for a rejection of the 'mind' of the flesh – the values and attitudes that are characteristic of those who live 'according to the flesh' (8:5–8).

Holiness of life is not simply attained by moral effort nor even by striving to keep the law of God. It is not even a matter of 'letting go and letting God'. Practical holiness involves 'putting to death' in our lives what God has already sentenced to death on the cross ('mortification') and living out the new life given to us by the indwelling Christ ('vivification' or 'aspiration'). Human effort is required, but not apart from, nor distinct from the activity of God's Spirit, who subdues the flesh as we mortify it in his power, and as we set our minds upon the things of the Spirit.

In short, the imperative for holy living in 8:12–13 is grounded in the fact that 'the Spirit of holiness' (1:4) has taken possession of us, demanding our continuing 'yes' to 'God's liberating and vivifying activity in past, present and future' (*cf.* 8:1–11; Deidun 1981: 80). The Spirit empowers us to walk in God's way and to counteract sin.

Conclusion

The rest of Paul's teaching about the work of the Spirit in Romans 8 will be my starting-point in the next chapter. There we will consider the themes of glorification, transformation and spiritual growth. My primary concern in this chapter has been to show how the death and resurrection of Jesus are the key to Paul's teaching about the Christian life in Romans 6 – 8.

When we are joined to Christ by faith, we experience the benefits of his death for sin and the liberating Spirit of our resurrected Lord. We are sanctified by the same redemptive work that makes it possible for us to be delivered from God's condemnation and stand before him as justified sinners. When Paul talks about dying together with Christ and being raised together with him (Rom. 6:1–11), *he expresses the notion of sanctification we have seen elsewhere in his writings*, without specifically using the terminology.

The present and the future dimensions of our sanctification are brought about by Jesus' dying and rising for us. But our present experience is one of tension and incompleteness as we await entire sanctification with the resurrection of our bodies. The positive consequences of our union with Christ are that we belong to God (6:12–13, 21), or to the one raised from the dead (7:4), and that we are 'in the Spirit' (8:9–13). Negatively, we must continue to struggle with sin and the flesh, as long as we remain in this body.

Calvin rightly perceived the importance of 'mortification' and 'vivification' as the essential demand arising from union with Christ in his death and resurrection. This is not only highlighted in Romans 8:12–13 (reflecting 6:11–13 in different terms), but also in Colossians 2:20 – 3:17 (*cf.* Eph. 4:22 – 5:20). Practical holiness means working out in everyday life and relationships the moral consequences of our union with Christ. In short, mortification brings us into conformity with Christ.[48] But we must beware of a rigour and intensity in this regard which gives the impression that the Christian life is more struggle than fulfilment, more depressing than hopeful.

Most importantly, Calvin noted the way Paul's *eschatology* controls his doctrine of sanctification. This view has not always been grasped by other writers on the theme. Although we participate by faith in all the benefits of Christ's death and resurrection, we must be content here and now to share visibly in the pattern of Christ's death rather than in the pattern of his glory. 'For the Spirit dispenses a power whereby they may gain the upper hand and become victors in the struggle', says Calvin. 'But sin ceases only to reign; it does not also cease to dwell in them' (*Inst.* 3.3.11).[49]

Paul's argument in Romans 6:1 – 8:13 establishes Christians as beneficiaries of Christ's death and resurrection, called to live in this age as those who belong to the age to come. Living by the power of his Spirit, however, we must do battle with the flesh, until God's purpose for us is consummated in our resurrection to glory.

Chapter Six

Transformation, renewal and growth

Victor Furnish, a contemporary ethicist, writes vigorously against the notion that sanctification means progress on our part:[1]

> If 'progress' is to include the idea of increasing 'achievement', then Paul allows no progress. The idea of progressive achievement supposes that there is some program of action which can be ultimately accomplished, such as full compliance with a law or full correspondence to a pattern or example. But nothing of the sort exists for Paul. Moreover, such could not be appropriated to his preaching, which constantly insists that fullness of life is not attained but given, and that Christian obedience is not an expression of man's effort gradually to realize his own innate potentialities, but an ever repeated response to the ever newly repeated summons of God. It has been seen that this is precisely the meaning of the 'sanctified' life – a life given over anew to the service of God (Furnish 1968: 239–240).

Although Paul does not describe it as such, his call to live as those 'brought from death to life' (Rom. 6:12–13), and as those 'led by the Spirit of God' (8:12–14), is effectively a call for ongoing repentance. This is what Furnish means by 'an ever repeated response to the ever newly repeated summons of God'. There can be no hiding from God's will and no compromise with the flesh. A sanctified life will continue to express what it means to be in an eternal relationship with the Holy One, through the work of his Son and by the gift of his Spirit.[2]

If the Holy Spirit is in charge, however, should we not expect progress in the sanctified life? As noted previously, God produces the fruit of sanctification in those who 'pursue' holiness (*e.g.* Gal. 5:16–26). Paul anticipates progress, but not simply as a result of human achievement. This chapter examines what the New Testament says about renewal in the image and likeness of God, transformation, glorification and growth. These themes are often included by theologians under the heading of sanctification. They are clearly an important dimension to the Bible's teaching about the Christian life, but how are they related to the view of sanctification that I have so far presented?

Glorified with Christ

As Paul continues to explain the work of the Holy Spirit in Romans 8:14–30, he shows how the privileges promised to Israel belong to those who are in Christ. Contrary to the understanding of his Jewish contemporaries, Paul insists that it is not faithfulness to the law that marks out the children of God but life 'in the Spirit' (as defined in 8:9–13). As many as are under the compulsion and direction of the Spirit of Christ are now 'sons of God' (8:14, Gk. *huioi theou. Cf.* Ex. 4:22–23; Je. 31:9; Ho. 1:10; 11:1).[3] This leads Paul to discuss the privileges of 'sonship', culminating in the promise of being 'glorified together with (Christ)' (8:17, Gk. *syndoxasthōmen*). But what does he mean by glorification? Is it a purely future experience or does it have a present dimension? And what is the link between suffering and glorification in the apostle's thinking?

The Spirit of adoption

The Spirit we have received is not a spirit of slavery, leading us to 'fall back into fear', but the Spirit who brings about our 'adoption' (Gk. *huiothesia*) as God's children (8:15; *cf.* Gal 4:5; Eph. 1:5). When the Spirit enables us to cry 'Abba! Father!', using the distinctive prayer language of Jesus himself, we are assured that we participate in Jesus' sonship. God's Spirit bears witness with our own spirit that we are truly 'children of God' (8:16, Gk. *tekna theou*).[4]

The idea of being God's children leads directly into the subject of our inheritance and our hope (8:17a). In Jewish thinking, Israel was God's inheritance (*e.g.* Dt. 32:9; 1 Ki. 8:51, 53; 2 Ki. 21:14; Is. 63:17), and this was confirmed by the fact that God gave them the land as their inheritance (*e.g.* Gn. 15:7; 17:8;

Nu. 34:2; Is. 60:21). In later Judaism, the language of inheritance was used to describe the life and situation of God's people in the age to come.[5] Paul's point is that *Christians* are now 'heirs of God', inheriting everything promised by God to his children (*cf.* Gal. 4:7; Eph. 1:14; Tit. 3:7).[6] The fact that we are 'joint heirs with Christ' is a reminder that we only enjoy the divine inheritance through Christ, who has already entered into it. Our 'sonship' and our 'inheritance' depend on our relation to him.

Suffering and glory

Participation in Christ's glorious inheritance, however, is conditional. We are joint heirs with Christ 'if, in fact, we suffer with him so that we may also be glorified with him' (8:17b).[7] Paul knows nothing of a Christian who does not suffer with Christ (*cf.* Acts 14:22; Phil. 1:29; 2 Tim. 3:12). But what is the nature of the suffering he has on view and what is its point and purpose? We have already noted the need for ongoing conformity to the death of Jesus in the moral life of believers (Rom. 6:3–13; 8:12–13). This has been characterized as repentance or mortification, which is a true sign of faith in the gospel. Paul could also have in mind the suffering of persecution. This is a logical consequence of confessing Christ in a world which does not choose to know him (*cf.* 8:35–36; 2 Cor. 4:7–12; Acts 14:22). But the following passage suggests that an even broader concept of suffering with Christ is in view.[8]

The children of God are caught up in the suffering of the whole created order (8:18–23). God himself subjected the creation to futility because of human sin (*cf.* Gn. 3:17–19). He put it in bondage to decay, until it could share in 'the freedom of the glory of the children of God' (8:21). Paul indicates that the Old Testament hope of a renewed creation, set free from suffering, corruption and death (*e.g.* Is. 11:6–9; 65:17–25; 66:22), will be fulfilled when Christians are resurrected and experience the redemption of their bodies. Creation itself must be redeemed so that redeemed humanity may have a fitting environment in which to live.[9]

Meanwhile, we are caught up with the 'groaning' of creation, as it 'waits with eager longing for the revelation of the children of God' (8:19). Christians must suffer like other people in 'this present time', but they do so with the knowledge that they are destined to share the liberation of the age to come. Once again Paul highlights the tension for believers caught in the overlap of the ages. 'We ourselves, who have the first fruits of the Spirit, groan inwardly while we wait for adoption, the redemption of our bodies' (8:23). God's final harvest is under way and we have the Holy Spirit as the 'first fruits' of what is to come. But the marvellous gift of God's Spirit actually causes us to cry with a deeper sense of distress and longing for the realization of our hope (*cf.* 8:26).

Suffering can be a means of confirming faith, producing endurance, proving character, and strengthening hope (5:3–4). But it can only be so for those who are convinced of God's promises and have that hope of sharing his glory in the first place (5:2).[10] Suffering with Christ in the broadest sense means being *conformed to the pattern of his earthly life,* which was to experience suffering as the preliminary and pathway to glory (*cf.* Phil. 3:10, 'becoming like him in his death'). We become more like Jesus when we learn to endure temptation, persecution and physical suffering, with patience and persistence, trusting in God for comfort and deliverance. Suffering for believers is therefore a means by which he fixes our hearts more firmly on 'the glory about to be revealed to us' (8:18).

The glorification of God's children

When Old Testament writers speak of the revelation of 'the glory of the LORD' (Heb. *kᵉbôḏ ᵃdōnāy*), they refer to God's *visible and active presence.*[11] This was recognized in creation (Ps. 19:1; Is. 6:3), but supremely experienced in God's great acts of salvation for Israel (Ex. 14:17–18; Ps. 96:3; Is. 40:3), and in the tabernacle or temple worship that he ordained for his people (Ex. 40:34–35; 1 Ki. 8:10–11; Ps. 26:8). In the last days, a full manifestation of God's glory was expected to consummate his purposes for Israel and convert the nations (Is. 60:1–2; Ezk. 39:21–22; Ps. 96:3–9; Hab. 2:14; Zc. 2:5–11).

In the intertestamental period there was much interest in this eschatological perspective. It was believed that Adam and Eve, who were created in the image and likeness of God (Gn. 1:26–27), shared something of God's glory, but lost what they had because they rebelled against him (*cf. Gen. Rab.* 12:6; *Apoc. Mos.* 21:6). Hence Paul's declaration that all have sinned and 'lack' the glory of God (Rom. 3:23; *cf.* 1:21–23). Judaism expected that the elect would inherit all the glory of Adam in the new age, experiencing the glory of God in such a way that they would be transformed by it.[12]

New Testament writers similarly view the future in terms of sharing God's glory (e.g. Rom. 5:2; 8:18; Heb. 2:10; 1 Pet. 5:1, 10). But they see this becoming a reality for us through Jesus Christ, who is the ultimate revelation of the glory of God (*e.g.* Jn. 1:14; 2 Cor. 4:4–6). He alone fulfilled God's purpose in making men and women in his own image. As the resurrected and ascended Lord, he is able to 'transform the body of our humiliation that it may be conformed to the body of his glory' (Phil. 3:21; *cf.* 1 Cor. 15:42–49). Bodily resurrection with Christ will mean having the glory-image fully restored in us, so that we are conformed in every way to the image of God's Son, in life and character (Rom. 8:29; 2 Cor. 3:18; Eph. 5:27; 2 Thes. 2:14).

Far from hindering our salvation, the troubles of this life are helps to it, since they continue to focus our faith on God's promises. In his providence, 'all things work together for good for those who love God, who are called according to his purpose' (Rom. 8:28). With these words, Paul introduces a magnificent outline of God's 'purpose' that ties together much of his thinking in Romans 8.

> For those whom he foreknew he also predestined to be conformed to the image of his Son, in order that he might be the firstborn among many brothers. And those whom he predestined he also called; and those whom he called he also justified; and those whom he justified he also glorified (8:29–30, NRSV modified).

Before they knew him and loved him, God 'foreknew' and called those who would be his people. Foreknowledge is a way of speaking about God's gracious, sovereign choice (*cf.* Rom. 11:2; 1 Pet. 1:2, 20).[13] He not only chose them but also determined in advance that they might be 'conformed to the image of his Son' (Gk. *symmorphous tēs eikonos tou hiou autou*). Such language recalls the teaching that we were created 'in the image of God' (Gn. 1:26–27). As noted previously, Jesus alone has fulfilled God's purpose in making humanity in his own image. Only when we share in his bodily resurrection will we be truly conformed to his image as the glorified Son of God (*cf.* Phil 3:21, Gk. *symmorphon*).

It is possible, however, that Romans 8:29 is thinking more particularly about the growing conformity of believers to Christ in suffering and obedience. That is suggested by the preceding context (8:17–28). The next verse then picks up the theme of glorification again, detailing how God's plan for us is consummated (8:30). Yet there is a sense in which glorification covers our present and our future experience as Christians. Through the Spirit, Christ as 'the firstborn' shares the glory of 'sonship' with those who have been justified by faith (8:15). But the full benefits of adoption are for those resurrected in glory with him (8:23).[14]

When Paul proclaims that those whom God justified 'he also glorified' (8:30, Gk. *kai edoxasen*), the aorist tense views our glorification as completed. God's purpose was fulfilled when Christ was glorified and in him our glorification has already been accomplished. The future for those who trust in Christ has already been decided. We are called to live within the framework of the divine plan, which stretches from eternity to eternity. Knowing what God has already done and what he intends to do, we are summoned in various ways to live a holy or sanctified life. To borrow the words of the apostle John, 'all who have this hope in him purify themselves, just as he is pure' (1 Jn. 3:3).

Conclusion

Being conformed to the pattern of Christ's suffering and obedience is central to Paul's view of the Christian life. Such a lifestyle reflects the reality of our union with Christ as those who have been justified and sanctified by faith. The emphasis in Romans 8:17–30 is not so much on becoming like Christ in his glorified state as identifying with him in his suffering. When we learn to submit to God's will with patience and hope, trusting that he is working out his good purpose for us, we are being conformed to the likeness of Christ in his suffering and death (8:28). This is God's pattern for those who would ultimately be glorified with Christ.[15]

Glorified by the Spirit

In 2 Corinthians 3:18, there is a classic statement about the transforming work of the Holy Spirit in all who turn to Christ. Here the concept of glorification is closely linked with the *present* activity of God in the lives of Christians.

And all of us, with unveiled faces, seeing the glory of the Lord as though reflected in a mirror, are being transformed into the same image from one degree of glory to another; for this comes from the Lord, the Spirit.

This verse forms the climax to a complex argument about the glory of the New Covenant. So we must first examine the context before focusing on this key verse.

The glory of gospel ministry

Against those who questioned his competence and the effectiveness of his ministry, Paul argued that the Corinthians were his greatest testimonial (3:1–6). The unmistakable result of his ministry in their lives was *the working of God's Spirit*. He needed no 'letters of recommendation', because the Corinthians were his 'letter', 'written not with ink but with the Spirit of the living God, not on tablets of stone but on the tablets of human hearts' (3:3). Paul's language here once again echoes the promises of Jeremiah 31:33 and Ezekiel 36: 26–27. Consequently, he claims that God has made him competent as one of the 'ministers of a new covenant, not of letter but of spirit' (3:6; *cf.* Rom 7:6).

The apostle goes on to develop a contrast between the veiled character of the Old Covenant and the openness of the New Covenant, which brings greater boldness and the hope of real transformation for all. Far from belittling the Old Covenant, he insists that it had its own glory. That glory has nevertheless been surpassed by the glory of the New Covenant.[16] By implication, his own ministry as 'the ministry of the Spirit' is a revelation of the greater glory of the New Covenant (3:8).

The difference between the two covenants and the ministries associated with them is illustrated with reference to Exodus 34:29–35. When Moses came down from Mount Sinai, with the tablets of the law in his hand, his shining face was a sign that he had truly been with the Lord and that the revelation he brought was divinely inspired. Although the people were afraid to draw near to him when his face was unveiled, Moses encouraged them to do so as a sign of God's continuing desire to communicate with them. He only put on the veil when he was *not* acting as a mediator.

According to Paul, the genuine glory of the Old Covenant was indicated by the fact that Israel could not continue to gaze at the unveiled face of Moses (2 Cor. 3:7). The inadequacy was not in the law but in the people to whom it was given (*cf.* Rom. 7:7–13). Something had to be done to enable sinful men and women to approach God directly and be able to gaze at the glory of God in an uninterrupted way. Indeed, this glorious revelation was fraught with danger for rebellious Israel: it became a ministry of death (3:7) and condemnation (3:9)

Furthermore, the glory associated with Moses and his revelation was fading, pointing beyond itself to a greater and lasting revelation of the glory of God (3:10–11). That greater glory comes from the ministry of the Spirit (3:8) and the ministry of justification (3:9). Such blessings flow from the death and resurrection of the Lord Jesus Christ and the ministry of the gospel, a ministry that has to do with the direct and permanent access to God which Jesus provides (3:12–14). It gives believers the hope of experiencing the glory of God themselves and great boldness to keep on drawing near to God through Jesus.

Paul first indicates why he can personally adopt a 'bold' style of ministry, speaking the truth in Christ without fear or reserve. 'We act with great boldness' (3:12, Gk. *parrēsia*), he says, because of the hope which the New Covenant gives.[17] His own freedom of speech in proclaiming and defending the gospel is in view here (*cf.* 2:17; 4:1–2) But the contrast in the passage that follows is 'not that between Paul and Moses, nor that between Christians and Moses, but that between the Christians – even those in Corinth! – and the Israelites, both of Moses' day and Paul's' (Wright 1991: 180).[18] Paul moves from affirming the dignity of his own office to speak of the status and hope of Christians generally.

The function of Moses' veil was actually misunderstood by Israel – because 'their minds were hardened' (3:14). Speaking from his own experience as a Jew, Paul claims that, 'to this very day, when they hear the reading of the old covenant, that same veil is still there, since only in Christ is it set aside'. Here he has transferred the veil from Moses' face to the reading of Moses' words in the synagogue. This 'veil' prevents the Israelites from understanding the law and seeing that there is a greater revelation of the glory of the Lord to be received and experienced in Jesus the Messiah. They imagine that the Old Testament is the final and most glorious revelation of the glory of the Lord.

Only in the Messiah is the veil removed (3:15–16), when people turn to Jesus, recognizing in him the ultimate revelation of God. The transformation of Moses' face actually pointed forward to the transformation effected in the lives of all who turn to God in Christ and receive his life-giving Spirit. What happened to Moses is now possible for *all* who believe the gospel about Jesus and are drawn by his Spirit into the fellowship of his people. Those who are in Christ are '*unveiled* precisely because their hearts are *unhardened* (3:1–3, 4–6)' (Wright 1991: 183). They have an openness to God which should make them receptive to the ministry of the Spirit which comes from people like Paul (*cf.* 3:8)!

The transforming power of God's Spirit

'Now the Lord is the Spirit', Paul continues, 'and where the Spirit of the Lord is, there is freedom' (3:17). 'The Lord' to whom he refers in 3:17–18 will be the Lord encountered by Moses on Mount Sinai, now revealed as the Lord Christ through the Holy Spirit. 'The Spirit, who applies the work of Christ to the life of the believer, is the key to the eschatological experience of God's presence' (Fee 1994: 312).[19] Where the Spirit of the Lord is, there is freedom (*cf.* Rom. 8:2, 21) – freedom to approach God 'with unveiled faces, seeing the glory of the Lord as though reflected in a mirror', and freedom to be transformed by that vision 'into the same image, from one degree of glory to another' (3:18).

All believers under the New Covenant can have an uninterrupted vision of the glory of God and the 'boldness' of approach enjoyed by Moses. There is no place for any spiritual élite in the New Testament. 'Seeing the glory of the Lord as though reflected in a mirror', however, suggests that Christians do not yet behold God directly (*cf.* 1 Cor. 13:12).

> Such direct vision is not for this world. They see his glory in a glass; in fact, what they perceive is the knowledge of the glory of God in the face of Jesus Christ (Barrett 1973: 125).[20]

From what Paul goes on to say in 4:4–6, this happens through the proclamation of 'the gospel of the glory of Christ, who is the image of God' (Gk. *eikōn tou theou, cf.* Col. 1:15).[21]

Transformation is the miracle we *all* experience as a result of seeing the glory of God in the face of Jesus Christ. The verb that Paul uses (Gk. *metamorphoumetha*) means 'to remodel' or 'to change into another form' (Behm 1967: 755).[22] Not just the outward appearance but the essential person is being changed. Linked with the expression 'the same image' (Gk. *tēn autēn eikona*), this verb indicates that we are changed into the likeness of Christ, who is himself the true image of God. In Christ we see not only the radiance of God's glory but also the true image of humanity. Into that one image we are all being transformed *together* (*cf.* Rom. 8:29; 1 Cor. 15:49; Col. 3:10).[23]

The passive 'we are being transformed' emphasizes that this is God's work in us ('all this comes from the Lord [who is] the Spirit'). Even though Paul uses a term much employed in the Hellenistic mystery religions, there is a vast difference in the way he conceives transformation taking place. It is effected by God, not by us. It is effected by gazing at Christ in the gospel, not by oft-repeated ritual. 'Mystical deification finds no place; the change into the likeness of Christ (*cf.* also Rom. 8:29) is a re-attainment of the divine likeness of man at creation' (Behm 1967: 758).[24]

'From one degree of glory to another' [Gk. *apo doxēs eis doxan*] literally means *from the present state of glory to the glory experienced when our bodies are redeemed* (*cf.* Rom. 8:21, 23).[25] The present tense of the verb 'to transform' suggests that the change is ongoing and progressive. On the other hand, we must keep in view the disjunction between this age and the next, which death brings for all except those who are alive at the time of Christ's return (*cf.* 1 Cor. 15:50–53; 1 Thes. 4:15–18). Paul does not confuse the initial stage of spiritual life with its perfection in the future. The link between now and then is 'pneumatological or Christological rather than anthropological. It resides in the possession and activity of the Spirit, not in the persistence of an immortal ego' (Harris 1983: 148).[26]

The Spirit's present work in us is a sign of the overlap of the ages and a pledge of ultimate transformation (2 Cor. 1:21–22; 5:5). As the element of continuity between this age and the next, the Holy Spirit prepares us for the climactic transformation that will mark the end of the process at the resurrection. But the picture is not a simple one of 'becoming more and more like Christ every day'. Progress is rarely in a straight line. Apart from the struggle between flesh and Spirit that we all experience, psychological damage from our past can be inhibiting and slow to heal. When change does not take place at the rate they desire, Christians ought not to be in bondage to guilt.

The reality is that 'we ourselves, who have the first fruits of the Spirit, groan inwardly while we wait for adoption, the redemption of our bodies' (Rom. 8:23; *cf.* 7:24–25). Spirit-filled Christian living cannot simply be equated with perfectionism or triumphalism. The Spirit inspires us to 'groan in labor pains', with the whole created order (Rom. 8:22), as we wait for God's new creation to be consummated. In short, there are two stages of the Spirit's work alluded to in 2 Corinthians 3:18.

> There is the ongoing present metamorphosis of character, and also the creation of the final "degree of glory" when Christians come to bear perfectly the image of the man from heaven (Rom. 8:29; 1 Cor. 15:49)' (Harris 1983: 149).

Conclusion

Glorification in a moral or spiritual sense is taking place here and now. It is an anticipation of what takes place when we meet Christ face to face, though there is no simple continuum of progress from regeneration to ultimate glorification. It is the Lord himself, present and active in our lives through his Spirit, who brings about this transformation. Put another way, Christ is 'being formed' in all who belong to him (Gal. 4:19, Gk. *morphōthē*). But we await the consummation of this at the resurrection.

2 Corinthians 3:18 gives us confidence in God and what he is presently doing in our lives. Instead of focusing on our failures and lack of progress, we are to fix our gaze on Christ (*cf.* Col. 3:1–4; Heb. 3:1; 12:2), not being distracted by anyone or anything else. There is no other genuine pathway to glory and change. In practical terms this means seeking to know him better from the Scriptures and making that the focus of our prayers. It means opening ourselves to the ministry of his Spirit in the fellowship of believers and trusting God to complete his

work in us (*cf.* Phil. 1:6). It means working out the practical implications of our salvation in day-to-day living, knowing that God is at work in us, enabling us 'both to will and to work for his good pleasure' (Phil. 2:12–13).[27]

As with the offer of salvation in the first place, we are totally dependent on God's grace for transformation, especially as we face the possibility of death. There is no programme of sanctification or glorification we can effect for ourselves. There is no way of hurrying-up God's work in us. We are called to live the sanctified life with faith, repentance and obedience, trusting the Spirit to continue and complete his great work of glorification.

Renewed by the Spirit

Several New Testament texts employ the language of renewal to describe what God is presently doing in the lives of his people. Only in Titus 3:5 is the Holy Spirit explicitly mentioned in this connection, but the Spirit's work is implied in other key texts (Rom. 12:2; 2 Cor. 4:16; Col. 3:10). An important link with the Spirit's transforming activity in 2 Corinthians 3:18 is forged by the use of the imperative 'be transformed' (Gk. *metamorphousthe*) in Romans 12:2. To these passages we now turn, to reflect on the nature of this renewal.

Regeneration and renewal

According to Titus 3:5–7, salvation is emphatically 'not because of any works of righteousness that we had done'. In God's mercy, it is a matter of being 'justified by his grace', so that we might become 'heirs according to the hope of eternal life'. The blessings of salvation are actually conveyed to us 'through the washing of rebirth and renewal by the Holy Spirit [Gk. *dia loutrou palingenesias kai anakainōseōs pneumatos hagiou*], whom God poured out on us richly through Jesus Christ our Saviour' (my translation).

A reference to baptism may well be intended here. However, as in 1 Corinthians 6:11 ('you were washed', Gk. *apelousasthe*) and Ephesians 5:26 ('the washing of water by the word', Gk. *tō loutrō tou hydatos en rhēmati*), the cleansing portrayed in baptism, and promised in the gospel, will be what saves. In Titus 3:5, 'the washing of rebirth' (Gk. *loutrou palingenesias*, NRSV 'the water of rebirth') is a definitive, initiating work of the Spirit of God (*cf.* Jn. 3:5). Applying the cleansing benefits of Christ's sacrifice to the lives of believers (*cf.* Heb. 10:22), the Spirit makes them part of the whole recreative and regenerative work of God that Jesus made possible by his death and resurrection (*cf.* 2 Cor. 5:17; 1 Pet. 1:3, 23).[28] They become part of the new world or new creation that God is bringing to birth.

'Renewal by the Holy Spirit' (Gk. *anakainōseōs pneumatos hagiou*) is not simply another way of speaking about 'the washing of rebirth'.[29] From Paul's use of the language of renewal elsewhere, it appears to be a continuous and progressive activity, arising from regeneration. 'Only the Spirit's constant infusion of spiritual life (*cf.* Eph. 4:23) into the believer sustains the new resurrection life received at "rebirth" when the believer was raised with Christ' (Harris 1983: 147).[30]

Paul wanted Titus to use this teaching as the basis for exhorting the believers in Crete to 'devote themselves to good works' (Tit. 3:8). The motivation and power for living a new life come from knowing the gracious cleansing of God in Christ and the renewing presence of his Spirit.

The renewal of the mind

The renewal of the mind in Romans 12:2 is bound up with the challenge to present our bodies to God in Christ (12:1). As the gospel is understood and believed, we are motivated and enabled to present ourselves as a living sacrifice, 'holy and acceptable to God'. This self-offering can only be acceptable in the first place because of the atoning work of his Son. If the service of our lives is to be continually pleasing to him, however, our agenda must be this: 'Do not be conformed to this world, but be transformed by the renewing of your minds, so that you may discern what is the will of God – what is good and acceptable and perfect.'

Paul first warns against the danger of being 'conformed' (Gk. *syschēmatizesthe*) to the pattern of 'this world / age' (Gk. *tō aiōni toutō*). In effect, he recognizes 'the power of social groups, cultural norms, institutions, and traditions to mould the patterns of individual behavior' (Dunn 1988b: 712).[31] The passive here points to the effect that these structures can have on us: Christians can be squeezed into the world's mould in their thinking and behaviour. Like Jesus in John 17, however,

Paul does not demand escape from the world and its pressures. He calls for a life in this world that is impelled and controlled by other factors.

God's transforming work is the powerful alternative to the influence of the world (Gk. *metamorphousthe*). Although the Holy Spirit is not named here, the renewal of the mind would seem to be critical to his work in believers. The Christian is to yield to the Spirit of God and his direction, rather than to the influence of this age and its norms (*cf.* Rom. 8:13–14). As we allow ourselves to be moulded by the norms and patterns of 'the age to come', we exhibit to the world the certainty and the character of the coming order that has already been manifested in Jesus Christ our Lord.

Transformation of the life that is offered to God (12:1) takes place from within, by the renewal of the mind (12:2, Gk. *tē anakainōsei tou noos*). As the following clause indicates, Paul is thinking about the mind as the faculty which enables us to test or 'prove what God's will is'.[32] Elsewhere, the role that we must play in actively reflecting on what pleases God is amplified (*e.g.* Phil. 4:8; Eph. 5:17). Renewal of the mind makes it possible for us to go on discerning God's will and presenting ourselves for daily obedience in the face of countless pressures to do otherwise.

Paul's challenge implies that the human mind, apart from such renewal, is unable to guide and keep us in the life that is pleasing to God. That is certainly the conclusion he reaches earlier in Romans, where he asserts that, since humanity 'did not think it worthwhile [Gk. *ouk edokimasan*] to retain the knowledge of God, he gave them over to a depraved mind [Gk. *eis adokimon noun*], to do what ought not to be done' (1:28).[33] Despite their intellectual achievements, people live and act 'in the futility of their minds' (Eph. 4:17; *cf.* Col. 2:18; 1 Tim. 6:5; 2 Tim. 3:8; Tit. 1:15), until they come to know Jesus and are taught in accordance with the truth that is in him. Then it is possible for them to be renewed in the attitude or 'spirit' of their mind (Eph. 4:23, Gk. *tō pneumati tou noos*).

So the first two verses of Romans 12 are closely linked and together proclaim a reversal of the foolishness and rebellion depicted in Romans 1:18–32.[34] Paul's ethic is not law-determined but its objective is still 'the will of God'. If we seek to discover more closely what the apostle meant by 'the will of

God', it is clear that some measure of 'the good and well-pleasing' is given in the following chapters of Romans. Apostolic teaching will be the means of discerning the will of God for a whole range of life-situations.

The renewal of the 'inner person'

There were many things that might have made the apostle Paul lose heart. Misrepresentation, opposition from false teachers, persecution from unbelievers and various life-threatening situations all contributed to the hardships he endured. Explaining what it meant for him to be a minister of the New Covenant, however, he demonstrated why he did not crumble in the face of adversity. His perseverance flowed out of his understanding of what God was doing *through* him (2 Cor. 4:1–15) and *in* him (4:16–18). Clearly, what he says in this last paragraph has an application to Christians generally:

> Even though our outer nature is wasting away, our inner nature is being renewed day by day. For this slight momentary affliction is preparing us for an eternal weight of glory beyond all measure, because we look not at what can be seen but at what cannot be seen; for what is seen is temporary, but what cannot be seen is eternal. (4:16–18)

The contrast is literally between 'our outer person' (Gk. *ho exō hēmōn anthrōpos*) and 'our inner person' (Gk. *ho esō hēmōn*). This is not simply the body–soul or body–mind contrast that was so common in the ancient Greek world. Such expressions elsewhere in Paul's writings suggest that he is referring to 'the man of this age and the man of the age to come' (*cf.* Rom. 6:6; 7:22; Eph. 3:16; 4:22, 24; Col. 3:9) (Barrett 1973: 146).[35] Our total existence is considered from two different points of view. What we are 'in Adam' can only waste away and be destroyed. What we are 'in Christ' – and will be fully at the resurrection from the dead – is being 'renewed' in us day by day.

Although the Spirit is not identified as the agent of this renewal, he is soon mentioned as the first instalment of God's total gift of transformation in glory (2 Cor. 5:5, 'the Spirit as a guarantee', Gk. *ton arrabōna tou pneumatos*). The intervening context suggests that renewal means more than spiritual refreshment or inner healing. It is even more than the renewal of our thinking and behaviour. God is preparing *a new person for glory*, out of the ashes of the old. He uses 'the slight momentary affliction' of depression, anxiety, suffering, and decay to produce for us 'an eternal weight of glory beyond all measure' (2 Cor. 4:17; *cf.* Rom. 8:18). We are being transformed 'from one degree of glory to another' (3:18).

Our part in the process in 4:18 is to keep our eyes fixed on the things that are unseen (the age to come), rather than on what can be seen (the present age). It is a matter of continuing to hope in the resurrection of the body and the glory that will be ours when we are 'clothed with our heavenly dwelling' (5:2), 'swallowed up by life' (5:4). Faith in God and his promises is the key to 'being renewed day by day'.

Renewal of the image of God

Using an argument that is reminiscent of Romans 6:2–11, Paul tells the Colossians that they died with Christ and were raised with him (Col. 3:1–4; *cf.* 2:12–13, 20). 'Set your minds on things that are above, not on things that are on earth,' he continues, 'for you have died, and your life is hidden with Christ in God. When Christ who is your life is revealed, then you also will be revealed with him in glory.' Their minds, their aims, and their behaviour were to be centred on that heavenly realm where Christ reigns and where their lives truly belonged. This was another way of telling them that their present existence was to be determined by the age to come and the glory that is to be revealed when Christ appears.

What does this mean in practical terms? As in Romans 8:12–13, Paul tells his readers that they are to 'put to death' (Col. 3:5, Gk. *nekrōsate*) or 'get rid of' (3:8, Gk. *apothesthe*) everything associated with the old life or 'the old person' in Adam (3:9, Gk. *ton palaion anthrōpon*).[36] Since they *are* new persons in God's sight, they are to *live* like new persons. Radical repentance is called for, with specific sins being named as being totally out of place in the life of God's holy people: fornication, impurity, passion, evil desire, greed, anger, wrath, malice, slander and abusive language (3:5–9). 'These are the ways you also once followed when you were living that life,' Paul admits, 'but now you must get rid of all such things' (3:7–8).

A twofold reason for the abandonment of such behaviour is

then given: 'seeing you have stripped off the old self' with its practices (3:9, Gk. *apekdysamenoi ton palaion anthrōpon*) and 'have clothed yourselves with the new self' (3:10, Gk. *endysamenoi ton neon*). The Gk. participles here refer to what happens when people turn to Christ and are baptized into his death (2:11–14; *cf.* Rom. 6:3–6).[37] When Jesus was crucified, 'the old self with its practices' was sentenced and condemned. When we turned to Christ, we turned our back on everything condemned by God. Paul's desire is that the repentance which characterizes the beginning of the Christian life should now be expressed in a thoroughgoing and continuing way.

Genuine repentance, however, is not simply a matter of turning from evil with sorrow. It is a matter of turning to God in Christ and placing one's life under his rule and control (*cf.* Rom 6:12–13). In place of the 'old self', believers put on 'the new self, which is being renewed in knowledge according to the image of its creator' (3:10; *cf.* Gal. 3:27). Consequently, 'as God's chosen ones, holy and beloved', Christians are to go on clothing themselves with the graces which are characteristic of that 'new self' or 'new man' (3:12–17). A simple parallel to the argument of Colossians 3 is found in Romans 13:14, where the apostle says, 'put on the Lord Jesus Christ, and make no provision for the flesh, to gratify its desires'.

Two things are of special note in Paul's presentation of the Christian life in Colossians 3. First, there is the affirmation that God's chosen ones are already 'holy and beloved' (3:12). This picks up the note of definitive sanctification observed elsewhere. Those who are holy, by God's calling and enabling, are to live out the implications of that holy status. Secondly, the basis for progress and change is the decisive 'putting off' of the old person in Adam and 'putting on' of the new person in Christ, which marked the beginning of their new relationship with God. For our part, renewal means continually going back to the beginning and expressing each day what it means to be a new person in Christ.

As noted in the previous chapter, Paul's thinking about the two 'men' has its basis in the Adam–Christ contrast of Romans 5:12–21 (*cf.* 1 Cor. 15:45–49). Foundationally, the 'new man' has a corporate reference. It is a way of speaking about *the new humanity in Christ*. This is confirmed by statements about the abolition of racial, religious, cultural and social barriers in

131

Colossians 3:11 (where 'there is no longer Greek and Jew, circumcised and uncircumcised, barbarian, Scythian, slave and free; but Christ is all and in all!'). In this context, renewal refers to 'a corporate recreation of humanity in the Creator's image' (O'Brien 1982: 191). Nevertheless, an individual dimension to the renewing work of God is also indicated in the passage. Christians individually 'put on Christ' at conversion / baptism.

The regenerating work of the Holy Spirit begins a process of renewal, which changes the mind and heart of the 'inner person' or 'inner being' (Rom. 12:2; 2 Cor. 4:16; Eph. 3:16–17; *cf.* Rom. 7:22), 'according to the image of its creator' (Col. 3:10, Gk. *kat' eikona tou ktisantos auton*). With an allusion to Genesis 1:27, the point is made again that, because of human rebellion, God's intention to create humanity in his image is only fulfilled in Christ. God's recreation of humanity is in the pattern of his Son, who is his likeness absolutely (Col. 1:15; 2 Cor. 4:4; Phil. 2:6). Ephesians 4:24 similarly declares that the 'new man' is 'created according to the likeness of God in true righteousness and holiness' (Gk. *ton kata theon ktisthenta en dikaiosynē kai hosiotēti*). 'Christ the Son of God, is the uncreated one; but the reproduction of his likeness in his people is an act of divine creation' (Bruce 1984: 359).[38]

What the saints are continually to 'put on', therefore, is new for them and makes them new, but it is not a novelty with God. Here we need to think again in terms of Paul's inaugurated eschatology. Jesus Christ is the one who makes them new. While 'the "truth" of their renewal is already present "in Jesus" (4:21), the saints still need to be "transformed into the likeness" of the New Man (2 Cor. 3:18)' (Barth 1974: 510).[39]

This renewal takes place 'in knowledge' (Gk. *eis epignōsin*), according to Colossians 3:10. It is by increasing in the knowledge of God's character and will that we are changed (*cf.* Phil. 1:9–11; Col. 1:9–10). Such knowledge 'the old man' does not have. According to Ephesians 4:23, however, renewal takes place 'in the spirit of your minds' (Gk. *tō pneumati tou noos hymōn*). This suggests that the pattern, motivation and direction of our thinking needs to be changed. Only then will Christ's character be formed in us and our behaviour will reflect his direction and control (*cf.* Rom. 12:2).

Conclusion

What makes me a new person in Christ is essentially faith in God and his promises. The Spirit's ongoing task is to renew my 'mind' through the gospel and give me a new 'heart' to serve God in faith and obedience. Renewal of mind and heart transforms character and behaviour because of the central place that the mind has in the orientation, attitudes and beliefs of the human personality. Renewal is not simply at the rational level, though this is foundational to the whole process of moral renewal and change that is effected by the Spirit. In the final analysis, renewal is the present experience of glorification through the Spirit, anticipating the glorification that will come with the resurrection of our bodies. It is being conformed to the likeness of Christ, who is himself the image of God.

There are obvious points of contact between Paul's teaching about renewal and his doctrine of sanctification. Hence the inclusion of renewal and transformation under the heading of sanctification in many systematic theologies. In Scripture, however, renewal is a different way of speaking about God's plan for us, arising from his original purpose for humanity in creation. Sanctification is specifically associated with covenant theology and the notion of belonging to God because of the redemptive work of his Son. In its broadest sense, renewal is a more comprehensive term, covering what is meant by sanctification and glorification, but setting these themes in a creation–recreation framework.

It is vital that the New Testament's distinctive teaching about sanctification should not be lost, when seeking to blend these themes together. The Spirit's regenerative work brings us to faith in Jesus as Saviour and Lord. This sanctifies us by consecrating us to God in a new and exclusive relationship of heart-obedience. The Spirit's renewing work continues in us as we trust in what Christ has done for us and seek to reflect in our lives the practical consequences of our union with Christ in his death and resurrection. Put another way, the Spirit moves us and enables us to express the holiness which is required of those who have been sanctified in Christ.

In view of what I have said about sanctification and renewal here, and my comments about living under righteousness and in holiness in the previous chapter, I would modify my earlier diagram (see p. 94) to give this more complete summary of New Testament teaching:

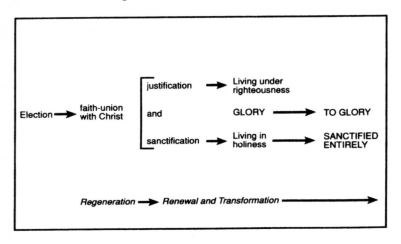

Growing together towards Christ

Some brief comments on the concept of growth in the New Testament are necessary to complete the picture. The language of growth is regularly used to describe the increase of the church in size, as well as its maturation and consolidation. A key to this growth is the word of God. In the Acts of the Apostles, for example, we are told that the word of God 'grew' and 'multiplied' (6:7; 12:24; 19:20). This is a way of describing the impact of the gospel on those who believed and were incorporated into the community of Christ. In 1 Corinthians 3:6–7, Paul makes it clear that *God* caused the Corinthian church to grow, as the apostle planted the seed of the gospel and Apollos watered it.

Ephesians presents the most developed picture of church growth. God is constructing a new 'household' of Jews and Gentiles who believe in Christ. 'In him the whole structure is joined together and grows into a holy temple in the Lord' (2:21). As the apostle moves on to consider how God achieves this purpose, various ministries of the word are identified as his gift, 'to equip the saints for the work of ministry, for building up the body of Christ' (4:11–12). This activity is to take place 'until we all come to meet the unifying faith and knowledge of the Son of God, the Perfect Man, the perfection of the Messiah who is the standard of manhood' (4:13, M. Barth's translation).[40]

The point of this verse is not so much to urge us to grow individually, so that each becomes a 'perfect man', nor even to suggest that the church must grow corporately into the likeness of Christ. The ministries given by the ascended Christ to his church (4:11) are designed for the important present activities mentioned in 4:12, 'until' (Gk. *mechri*) the people of God 'meet' perfection or maturity in the person of their Lord and share completely in his glory (4:13). Our ministry to one another should help us so to engage with Christ now that we are ready to meet him when he comes.

Inspired by sound teaching, the growth of the church 'toward him who is the head' takes place as members of the body of Christ 'speak the truth in love' to one another (4:14–16). Only by being led away from error and established in the truth can the body be sustained and kept in holiness, until it reaches the goal that has been set for it (4:13).

Paradoxically, growth comes *from Christ* (4:16, Gk. *ex hou*), to enable the whole church to grow up *into Christ* (4:15, Gk. *eis auton*). But we must each be active in the process. The body upbuilds itself in love 'as each part is working properly', because Christ is at work, joining and holding it together, providing sustenance to it 'through every contact, according to the needs of each single part' (M. Barth's translation).[41] Christians can only grow together towards Christ and the glory that is to come 'with a growth that comes from God' (Col. 2:19).

The New Testament elsewhere speaks of growth in faith (2 Cor. 10:15; 2 Thes. 1:3), in love (1 Thes. 3:12; 2 Thes. 1:3), and in 'the grace and knowledge of our Lord and Saviour Jesus Christ' (2 Pet. 3:18; *cf.* Col. 1:10). Like newborn infants, Christians are to long for 'the pure, spiritual milk', so that by it they may grow towards final salvation (1 Pet. 2:2). Such teaching is addressed to congregations as well as to the individuals within them. Spiritual growth is not something that is normally expected to take place in isolation from other believers.

In certain respects, then, the concept of growth is similar to that of renewal. It is the work of God through his word, moving us towards his ultimate goal for us in the new creation. But the particular point and purpose of this biblical terminology must not be obscured by confusing it with other terms. So, again, spiritual growth could be described as an important dimension to the sanctified life. But the link between the concepts must be carefully established. If we are definitively sanctified by the work of Christ and the gift of his Spirit, 'growth' in holiness will mean increasing and abounding in practical expressions of that status, calling and commitment which is already ours by God's grace.

Summary conclusions

1. The popular view that sanctification is a process of moral renewal and change, following justification, is not the emphasis of the New Testament. Rather, sanctification is primarily another way of describing what it means to be converted or brought to God in Christ and kept in that relationship. It would be more accurate to say that renewal and change flow from the regeneration and sanctification that God has already accomplished in our lives.

2. Sanctification is thus primarily the work of Christ on the cross and of the Holy Spirit through the word of the gospel, bringing us into an exclusive and dedicated relationship with God, as the holy people of the New Covenant. It is a concept with important, ongoing implications for the church, as well as for individual believers.

3. Although Paul speaks about being sanctified 'entirely' at the return of Christ (1 Thes. 5:23), he elsewhere uses the language of glorification for the final transformation of believers into the likeness of his glorified Son. Instead of speaking in terms of progressive sanctification, the New Testament more regularly employs the language of renewal, transformation and growth, to describe what God is doing with us here and now.

4. Although the language of glorification may be used to speak of the Spirit's present work in our lives (e.g. 2 Cor. 3:18), the New Testament offers no simple picture of daily progress to future glory. Flesh and Spirit are locked in a conflict that does not always see victory going to the one side. We are presently being conformed to Christ's sufferings so that we might share with him in the ultimate transformation of resurrection.

5. Sanctification is a vital aspect of God's total plan for renewing us and the whole creation. The call of Scripture is to live out the practical implications of our sanctification by

pursuing holiness as a lifestyle. We are to do this by looking back to the cross and forward to the resurrection, when by God's grace we will share his character and life completely. We are to grow in our knowledge of God and his will, so that we might better reflect his holiness in every aspect of our lives. We are to 'keep in step with the Spirit' (Gal. 5:25 NIV), so that the fruit of the Spirit may be revealed in us. As God's 'holy and beloved', we are to abandon the values, attitudes and practices that belong to the 'old self' and be clothed with 'the new self, which is being renewed in knowledge, according to the image of its creator' (Col. 3:10).

6. History shows that, when the terminology of sanctification is simply used to describe everything that happens to us after conversion, the definitive emphasis of the New Testament is soon obscured. The call to 'be holy' can so easily degenerate into a moralistic and perfectionist programme for believers to pursue. In New Testament terms, we are to live as those who have been brought from death to life, discharged from the law to belong to Christ, led by the Spirit in a continuing struggle with the flesh. We are to live with a confidence in what God has already done for us and trust in him to continue his transforming work in us until we see him face to face.

> Finish then thy new creation,
> pure and spotless let us be:
> let us see thy great salvation,
> perfectly restored in thee.
> Changed from glory into glory,
> till in heaven we take our place;
> till we cast our crowns before thee,
> lost in wonder, love and praise.
>
> *Charles Wesley*

Appendix A

The meaning of *hagiasmos* in the New Testament

The verb *hagiazein*, which is used twenty-eight times in the New Testament, may be translated 'to set apart, consecrate, hallow, sanctify, treat as holy'. God the Father is the implied or stated agent in some cases (Mt. 6:9; Lk. 11:2; Jn. 10:36; 17:17; Acts 20:32; 26:18; 1 Thes. 5:23; 1 Tim. 4:5), God the Son in other cases (Jn. 17:19; 1 Cor. 1:2; 6:11; Eph. 5:26; Heb. 2:11; 9:13; 10:10, 29; 13:12), and God the Holy Spirit in others (Rom. 15:16; 1 Cor. 6:11). Some form of self-consecration is implied by 2 Timothy 2:21, God is sanctified by the beliefs and actions of his people in 1 Peter 3:15 (*cf.* Mt. 6:9; Lk. 11:2), and the holy are exhorted to continue in holiness by Revelation 22:11.

Clear evidence for this verb and the noun *hagiasmos* outside biblical and ecclesiastical writings appears to be wanting. Greek religion already had the verb *hagizein* ('to hallow, make sacred') and associated terms such as *hagismos*, with distinctive technical meanings. When the adjective *hagios* ('holy') was appropriated in Jewish and Christian circles to represent different views of holiness, it appears that words with the added -*a*- were employed as substitutes for the familiar forms. These variants answered the traditional words in function, but were 'free from pagan association' (Moulton & Milligan 1930: 4).[1]

The adjective *hagios* ('holy') is employed some 233 times in the New Testament, mostly with reference to the Holy Spirit, to Jesus as 'the Holy One of God', and to saints or angels as God's 'holy ones'. The rare noun *hagiotēs* (Heb. 12:10; 2 Cor. 1:12 [only some MSS]) and the more common alternative *hagiōsynē* (Rom. 1:4; 2 Cor. 7:1; 1 Thes. 3:13) refer to the sanctity of God's character and life, which he shares with believers in some measure at the present time but fully and finally when they see him face to face.

Much more debatable is the meaning and application of the noun *hagiasmos*, which is used on ten critical occasions in the

139

New Testament. The following chart shows the various ways it is translated in three current English versions.

	NRSV	NIV	NASV
Rom. 6:19, 22	sanctification	holiness	sanctification
1 Cor. 1:30	sanctification	holiness	sanctification
1 Thes. 4:3	sanctification	be holy	sanctification
1 Thes. 4:4	holiness	in a way that is holy	sanctification
1 Thes. 4:7	holiness	to live a holy life	sanctification
2 Thes. 2:13	sanctification	through the sanctifying work	sanctification
1 Tim. 2:15	holiness	holiness	sanctity
Heb. 12:14	holiness	to be holy/holiness	sanctification
1 Pet. 1:2	sanctified	by the sanctifying work	by the sanctifying work

In a much-quoted article, Otto Procksch describes *hagiasmos* as 'a *nomen actionis*' (noun expressing action), derived from the verb *hagiazein*. Procksch argues that it means 'sanctifying', rather than 'sanctification' as a state or condition.[2] This particularly dynamic sense, however, is not reflected in the rare LXX usage to which he refers. There the noun means sanctification or consecration in a definitive, cultic sense (*e.g.* Jdg. 17:3; Ezk. 45:4; Am. 2:11; Sir. 7:31; 2 Macc. 2:17) or it is used adjectivally in a Hebraic construction like 'name of holiness' = 'holy name' (Sir. 17:10; *cf.* 2 Macc. 14:36; Rom. 1:4). In later Christian writings, the noun can refer to 'sanctity' as a divine quality or as a status which God gives to his people. In some texts it is also clear that a process of sanctification or consecration is in view (Lampe 1961: 17).[3]

Procksch rightly points to the foundational importance of Christ's atoning work in New Testament teaching about sanctification (1 Cor. 1:30). He also highlights the operation of the Holy Spirit, bringing that work into effect in believers (2 Thes. 2:13; 1 Pet. 1:2). Based on texts such as Romans 6:19, 22; 1 Thessalonians 4:3, 4, 7; and Hebrews 12:14, however, he asserts that *hagiasmos* is the 'moral goal' or 'moral form' which develops out of the atonement. Although he tries to take the diversity of New Testament usage seriously, this conclusion really does not follow from his opening insistence on the dynamic character of this noun.

The meaning of *hagiasmos* must first be determined by observing the way in which the verb *hagiazein* is employed by a particular writer. Hence my argument that *hagiasmos* in 1 Corinthians 1:30 is a reference to the work of sanctification mentioned in 1 Corinthians 1:2; 6:11. It is a way of describing the saving work of God in Christ, drawing people into an exclusive relationship with himself through the cross. The initiating work of the Holy Spirit, enabling faith in Christ as Saviour, is most obviously intended by the context in 2 Thessalonians 2:13 and 1 Peter 1:2. In such passages, the primary meaning is 'consecration'. Similarly, *hagiasmos* in Hebrews 12:14 must be understood with reference to the sanctifying work of Christ mentioned in Hebrews 2:11; 9:13; 10:10, 29; 13:12.

It must be acknowledged, however, that 'holiness' is a valid translation in certain contexts, where the state or condition resulting from a process of sanctification is implied.[4] This is most obviously so in 1 Timothy 2:15, where even the NASV in its desire for consistency of translation must render the noun 'sanctity'. It is also a possible nuance in Hebrews 12:14, where 'peace' and 'holiness' are the fruit of Christ's redemptive work, which believers are continually to 'pursue'.

Paul's first use of *hagiasmos* in 1 Thessalonians 4:3 could be taken as a synonym for 'holiness' in 3:13 (Gk. *hagiōsynē*), functioning as an equivalent for Old Testament declarations about holiness being the essential will of God for his people. Consistent with this understanding, 4:4 would then be saying that we are to to keep our bodies 'in holiness and honour' (Gk. *en hagiasmō kai timē*). In 4:7 Paul would then be stressing that God's elective call was not 'to impurity but in holiness' (Gk. *epi akatharsia all' en hagiasmō*).

On the other hand, this last text suggests that a different rendering of *hagiasmos* could be given throughout this passage.

God's will is 'sanctification' in the sense that he demands a consecrated lifestyle (4:3). We are to keep our bodies in a state of sanctification and honour (4:4) because that is the context or condition in which we were called (4:7). Holiness as a way of life flows from consecration to God in Christ.

Given Paul's usage of *hagiasmos* in these other contexts, it is unlikely that in Romans 6:19, 22 the primary meaning is progressive ethical renewal. As in 1 Thessalonians 4:7, 'holiness' or 'sanctification' is first presented as an alternative to 'uncleanness' (*akatharsia*) and 'lawlessness' (*anomia*, Rom. 6:19). It is the fruit that comes from presenting ourselves to 'righteousness' (*diakaiosynē*). Put another way, it is the immediate fruit of being set free from sin and becoming slaves to God, eternal life being the ultimate gift (Rom. 6:22). Sanctification as a dedicated state is most likely in view, though this condition in the New Testament clearly demands expression in holy living and a commitment to change.

In conclusion, where the context suggests that *hagiasmos* has the dynamic sense of 'sanctification', it must be interpreted in the light of the particular writer's use of the verb *hagiazein*. On the other hand, *hagiasmos* need not always be read in a dynamic sense. In some passages it is best understood as a state of holiness arising from God's consecrating work in Christ. The motivation and power to express that holiness is given to believers by the indwelling Holy Spirit.

Appendix B

Sanctification and God's law

John Calvin's influential thesis was that the Mosaic law was given for three reasons: to convict of sin, to restrain evil, and to teach and exhort God's servants to do his will.

> The third and principal use, which pertains more closely to the proper purpose of the law, finds its place among believers in whose heart the Spirit of God already lives and reigns (*Inst.* 2.7.12).[1]

Although they have the law written and engraved on their hearts and are moved by the Spirit to obey God, Calvin argues that Christians profit by the law in two ways. First, by using it 'to learn more thoroughly each day the nature of the Lord's will to which they aspire, and to confirm them in the understanding of it'. Secondly, 'by frequent meditation upon it to be aroused to obedience, be strengthened in it, and be drawn back from the slippery path of transgression'. Indeed, 'the law is to the flesh like a whip to an idle and balky ass, to arouse it to work'!

Ever since the Reformation, many have echoed this viewpoint, arguing that the law is one of the most important means whereby God produces the fruit of holiness in us.

> Though believers must not try to keep God's law as a means of earning their salvation, they are nevertheless enjoined to do their best to keep this law as a means of showing their thankfulness to God for the salvation they have received as a gift of grace (Hoekema 1987: 88).[2]

By his saving work in Christ, God takes possession of us and renews us through the operation of his word and his Spirit, but 'the law of God remains the standard of holiness for the New

Testament believer' (Ferguson 1988: 69).[3] Sanctification in its progressive dimension involves conformity to God's moral law.

This approach has often been criticized, however, for over-playing the role of the law in the life of the Christian and misreading the New Testament. 'The gospel is the source of holiness, the power of God unto salvation. It is not the law' (Forde 1988: 80–81).[4] 'To focus on the meaning of sanctification primarily in terms of performance instead of on the relational dimension of love makes it difficult to avoid Puritanical and moralistic attitudes' (Wood 1988: 84). 'True righteousness is not so much obedience to behavioral regulations as it is the living out of a new relationship with God – as his "sons", conformed to the likeness of his Son' (Fee 1994: 561).[5] The Mosaic law is no longer '*a direct and immediate* source of, or judge of, the conduct of God's people' (Moo 1993: 343).

From a New Testament point of view, it is important to give due weight to statements such as 'you are not under law but under grace' (Rom. 6:14), 'you have died to the law through the body of Christ' (Rom. 7:4), 'now we are discharged from the law, dead to that which held us captive' (Rom. 7:6) and Paul's claim that he was no longer personally bound to live as one 'under the law' (1 Cor. 9:20). It is unlikely that such passages refer simply to release from the law's condemnation or from a legalistic misunderstanding and abuse of the law.[6] It is also inadequate to interpret 'under the law' in sociological terms, as characterizing the form of life 'as it has been experienced within Judaism' (Dunn 1988a: 339).[7] The apostle is not reacting to human misunderstandings of the role of the law, but is speaking about the law '*as God gave it* and thus of the intended function of the law in salvation history' (Moo 1991: 405)[8]

'Law' and 'grace' are presented as contrasting salvation-historical powers by Paul, so that 'under the law' is another way of characterizing 'the old era'. There can be no final liberation from the power of sin without a corresponding liberation from the power and dominion of the law. Douglas Moo expresses the contrast in these terms:

> To be under the law is to be subject to the constraining and sin-strengthening regime of the old era; to be under grace is to be subject to the new era in which freedom from the power of sin is available (1991: 407).[9]

Yet Moo offers three important caveats to this explanation. First, the nature of Paul's salvation-historical scheme is such that 'a neat transfer into straightforward temporal categories is impossible' (1991: 407). People before the coming of Christ, while still 'bound' to the law, could escape its condemnation and power by relying on God's grace. People after the coming of Christ may still be subject to the law's condemnation and power. Secondly, unlike the other 'powers' of the old era (sin, the flesh and death), the law is not an intrinsically negative force. Despite its largely negative role in salvation-history, it is God's holy, just and good law (Rom. 7:7–12, 14). Thirdly, Paul is thinking of the Mosaic law as a *system* or *body*. We are free from the command-ments of the Mosaic law inasmuch as they are part of that system, but we cannot conclude that the believer has no obligation to any of the individual commandments of that law, 'insofar as they may be isolated from the system' (1991: 408).[10]

Christian interpreters agree that there is some discontinuity of the Sinai Covenant, now that the New Covenant has been inaugurated. The moot point is the degree of continuity and progression. Thomas Schreiner, for example, establishes from Galatians 3:15 – 4:7 and 2 Corinthians 3:4–18 that the Mosaic Covenant was a temporary provision, designed to last until the coming of the Messiah (Schreiner 1993: 123–143). The atoning work of Jesus and the descent of the Spirit marked the cessation but also the fulfilment of that covenant. Sacrifices and festivals are clearly fulfilled in Christ. Consequently, the observance of 'days and months and seasons and years' is not required of believers (Gal. 4:10). With the advent of the new era, Christians themselves become the temple of God, cleansed by faith in Christ and indwelt by the Holy Spirit. So purity laws no longer apply in a literal sense. Even the covenant sign of circumcision has a spiritual application in Christ (*e.g.* Rom. 2:28–29; Phil. 3:3). Laws given to distinguish Israel as a holy nation in a cultic or social sense are not binding upon the church, though they still have a revelatory or teaching function for us.[11]

Schreiner's inductive study of Paul, however, leads him to conclude that the moral norms or absolutes of the law still obligate Christians. The Old Testament command to love one's neighbour as oneself sums up the entire law, so that 'love is the fulfilling of the law' (Rom. 13:8–10; *cf.* Gal. 5:14). Love is clearly at the heart of Paul's ethic, but 'he does not allow love to float free at the ethical center without any articulation of definite requirements' (1993: 147).[12] Specific Old Testament commandments (*e.g.* Rom. 13:9; 1 Cor. 9:9–10; Eph. 6:2) and apostolic exhortations (*e.g.* Rom. 12:1 – 15:13; Gal. 5:13 – 6:10) provide *parameters for the expression of love by Christians*. Paul's exhortations can even affirm what the Mosaic law required, without quoting the law as an authority (*e.g.* 1 Cor. 6:9–10, 12–20; 10:14–22). Concrete demands do not diminish love or quench life in the Spirit, for the Spirit uses such demands to inform believers and enable them to please God.

Frank Thielman takes a different approach but reaches somewhat similar conclusions. He argues that, even in letters where the law is not explicitly addressed, Paul alludes to it, and 'his allusions reveal a pattern of thinking about the law which will reappear frequently in his other letters' (1994: 70). Thus, for example, the apostle's understanding of the identity of the Thessalonian community is patterned after the understanding of Israel's identity revealed in the Mosaic law (*e.g.* 1 Thes. 4:1–8). Nevertheless,

> . . . the lack of specific correlation between Paul's ethical admonitions and the behavior required of a sanctified Israel in the Mosaic law shows that for him many of the Mosaic law's specific requirements have dropped from view (1994: 79).[13]

Paul considered the law's demand for holiness to be authoritative, but he used the law to support this idea in a different way from the typical Judaism of his day. The pattern of teaching he gave to his converts absorbed elements of the Mosaic law and had some continuity with it. But 'the Sinaitic covenant as the sign of the election of God's people and as the definitive guide to their sanctity has come to an end' (1994: 213).

This is a complex issue and I have only briefly touched on some of the contentious points. Meditation on the Mosaic law is doubtless a means of learning more thoroughly 'the nature of the Lord's will', as Calvin suggested. But Matthew 5 and Paul's ethical teaching suggest that it is the law as interpreted and applied by Jesus and his apostles that should guide the Christian. For example, Jesus insists that the righteousness of the kingdom involves going beyond the literal demands of the law (Mt. 5:21–

30). Indeed, in certain cases he sets aside its specific commands and establishes the law's fundamental requirements in a new way (Mt. 5:33–42).

Using his own distinctive method of appeal, Paul warns about the need to avoid idolatry and sexual immorality in particular situations faced by his converts (*e.g.* 1 Cor. 5:1–8; 10:1–22). He incorporates arguments from the law but does not simply command obedience to its commands. In fact, although God's will is the object of a constant and repeated seeking, finding and doing for Paul, he refuses to identify it absolutely with the statutes of the law. Discerning God's will for our lives is a more complex issue than reflecting on the law of Moses, even though such reflection has a part to play.[14]

Calvin's view that the law is the means by which we are aroused, strengthened and kept from sin, seems to put the focus where the New Testament does not. What he says about the law is certainly applicable to Scripture as a whole, when it is understood and obeyed by Spirit-directed believers. But for Paul it is the knowledge of God in Christ that pre-eminently transforms and renews us (*e.g.* 2 Cor. 3:18; 4:6). The restraint of the law is not an adequate antidote to fleshly indulgence (*cf.* Rom. 7:7–25). It is only the life in Christ, lived in the power of the Holy Spirit, that can be the fulfilment of the law's requirement (*cf.* Rom. 8:3–4; 13:8–10).[15]

Put another way, Christians are not 'under the law' because they live under the lordship of Christ (*cf.* 1 Cor. 9:20–21). In fact, the apostle uses the paradoxical expression 'under Christ's law' (9:21, Gk. *ennomos tou Christou*, lit. 'in-lawed to Christ'), to counter any suggestion that he is promoting an antinomian libertinism. What the Mosaic law required is fulfilled in those who stand under the will or 'law' of God as revealed in Jesus Christ (*cf.* Gal. 6:2).[16] For all that, the evidence does not suggest that Paul's ethical teaching was meant to function as a nomistic system. The New Covenant form of God's law is:

> . . . not a code or series of commandments and prohibitions, but is composed of the teachings of Christ and the apostles and the directing influence of the Holy Spirit. Love is central to this law, and there is strong continuity with the law of Moses, for many specifically Mosaic commandments are taken up and

included within this 'law of Christ' (Moo 1993: 368).[17]

It would be inappropriate to conclude this discussion without mentioning another influential, contemporary approach. E. P. Sanders has shifted the centre of the discussion on Paul from justification and freedom from the law to the notions of 'getting in' and 'staying in' the covenant community.[18] The apostle is said to have used the term 'law' in at least two quite distinct contexts, 'one in discussing how one gets "in" (not by works of law), the other in discussing how one who is "in" behaves (he keeps the law)' (1983: 10).

Jews and Gentiles can only be 'righteoused' by faith in Christ, to quote Sanders' rendering of the passive form of the Greek verb *dikaioun*. By this means, they are cleansed and transferred from the state of sin to the new life in Christ. Once they are in the body of those who are to be saved, they must 'fulfil' the law to maintain their status and 'are judged according to how well they fulfil the law' (Sanders 1983: 112).[19]

According to Sanders, Paul never makes a theoretical distinction with regard to what aspects of the law are binding. On the other hand, he does make a *de facto* reduction of the law's demands on Christians in terms of the social distinctions created by circumcision, food laws and Sabbath (1983: 101–105).[20] The apostle to the Gentiles consciously deleted things from the law because of his conviction that all are to be saved on the same basis, but he nevertheless called for obedience to 'the whole law' (Gal. 5:14; *cf.* 1 Cor. 7:19). To some degree, then, the law still functions as law for the Christian and obedience is a condition for continuance in salvation.

Sanders' approach cannot be adequately assessed in the space of a few paragraphs. In offering these brief comments, I draw attention to the more extensive critique of others. Firstly, for Paul, 'getting in and staying in are covered by the seamless robe of faith as opposed to works, with the result that works come in as evidential rather than instrumental' (Gundry 1985: 12). We enter the New Covenant by God's grace but do so as God enables us to repent and believe. Although it is true that we are to persevere in that covenant by obedience, such obedience is the fruit of grace and is empowered by the indwelling Spirit of God (*cf.* Phil. 2:12–13; Eph. 2:10; Gal. 5:16–26).

Secondly, Paul's critique of Judaism and Judaistic Christianity was not simply due to a dispensational change in salvation-history, introduced by the coming of Christ. Significant evidence exists that Paul opposed a form of Jewish legalism or works-righteousness and did so because of the conviction 'that it would corrupt what he had come to believe concerning God's grace in Jesus Christ' (Gundry 1985: 37–38).[21]

Thirdly, Sanders' view of justification as a 'transfer' term is inadequate. The language is used by Paul in relation to the beginning of the Christian life and with reference to its evaluation and vindication at the final judgment (*e.g.* Gal. 2:16; Rom. 3:20). Paul's exclusion of justification by 'works of the law' must refer to both the present and the future.[22]

Fourthly, as I have argued in chapter five and in this appendix, Paul's view of the way the law is fulfilled is more complex than Sanders allows. The apostle does not simply modify the law's demands to meet the requirements of the Gentile mission. Furthermore, his *de facto* reduction of the law's demands goes much further that Sanders suggests. For Paul, the law is fundamentally fulfilled in the work of Christ and in the establishment of the church as the community of the new age, indwelt by the Holy Spirit. What eventuates, by the Spirit's enabling, is a newness of life and a pattern of obedience that enables Christians to fulfil what the Mosaic law essentially required.

Notes

Introduction

[1]The five contributors in Alexander's *Christian Spirituality* (1988) are S. B. Ferguson, G. O. Forde, E. G. Hinson, R. P. Spittler and L. W. Wood.

[2]Hoekema's *Saved by Grace* (1989) contains a revised and expanded version of his chapter 'The Reformed Perspective' in Dieter *et al* 1987: 61–90.

[3]Apart from his treatment of Romans 6, Hoekema (1989) does not adequately deal with the relationship between the definitive and the progressive aspects of sanctification. *Cf.* Murray 1977: 277–293.

[4]Bockmuehl (1988) shows how the soteriological and ethical dimensions of sanctification became separated in the thinking of later Christian writers. He then provides a brief historical survey of the way the theme has been understood and expounded. *Cf.* Van Rensburg 1967: 73–87.

[5]Porter (1993: 399) similarly concludes that 'if one must reduce sanctification to a single notion, it may be summarized in the idea that the believer *both* lives in holiness *and* grows into holiness'. I will be particularly concerned to test the notion of growing 'into holiness'.

1. The biblical starting-point

[1]A summary and assessment of various theologies of sanctification is found in Dieter *et al*, *Five Views on Sanctification* (1987), and in Alexander (ed.) *Christian Spirituality* (1988). *Cf.* the brief historical survey in Bockmuehl (1988: 614–615), and the theological assessment in Packer (1984: 121–164).

[2]The root *qdš* is probably derived from the stem *qd*, 'to cut', rather than from the stems *qd'* or *qdu*, 'to be pure or bright', which are known to us from the Arabic and Ethiopic. Although there were similar concepts in other ancient religions, Eichrodt (1961: 272) observes the distinctiveness of the OT in introducing 'a personal element into the theory of holiness'.

[3]Procksch (1964: 89–97) artificially separates 'the religious' from 'the ethical' in his reconstruction of the history of the use of holiness terminology in the Bible. Contrast the approach of Gammie (1989).

[4]Moses was personally confronted by the holiness of God in the incident with the burning bush (Ex. 3:1–5). As he learned the name of God and received the promises of God for Israel, he anticipated the experience of Israel in the exodus and at Mount Sinai (Ex. 19).

[5]Repetition of the word 'holy' is for the sake of emphasis here. In modern English we might say that he is 'utterly and completely holy'. Whereas God's glory is the manifestation of his character and presence in biblical thought, 'his holiness denotes his innermost and secret essence' (Procksch 1964: 93).

[6]A veiled messianic reference could be intended in Is. 6:13, but it is more likely that the 'holy seed' represents the remnant who will finally enjoy God's promises in the new Jerusalem.

[7]Dumbrell (1984: 84–90) provides an excellent discussion of Ex. 19:5–6, showing particularly how Israel was to exercise an 'Abrahamic role'.

[8]'Just as a priest is separated from an ancient society in order to serve it and serves it by his distinctiveness, so Israel serves her world by maintaining her distance and her difference from it' (Dumbrell 1984: 90).

[9]With reference to Exodus 19, Gammie (1989: 6–8) rightly points to the inadequacy of Rudolph Otto's famous classification of the five aspects of holiness. 'Nowhere does Otto sufficiently probe the notion that the holy calls for purity, cleanness, and that frequently purity is to be attained by means of separation' (7).

[10]The perspective that holiness is 'contagious' is given in Ex. 29:37 ('whatever touches the altar shall become holy'). Cf. Ex. 30:29; Lv. 6:18, 27. From 7:27–28 it appears that this transfer of holiness is not necessarily a good thing: objects had to be deconsecrated after contact with the holy. Cf. Wenham 1979: 121. On the holiness of objects and places in the OT, cf. Wright 1992: 239–243.

[11]Cf. Peterson 1992: 31–34.

[12]Lv. 20:7–8 shows 'human self-sanctification and God's sanctification of man as its cause, side by side, both the imperative and the indicative in dialectical harmony' (Bockmuehl 1988: 613).

[13]Note Wenham's whole discussion of the holy–common, clean–unclean distinctions (1979: 18–25), based on the work of Douglas (1966). Cf. also Wright 1992: 244–248.

[14]Eichrodt (1970: 496–497) rightly argues that there is no mistaken identification of Israel's honour with God's honour here: 'If Israel can still possess any sort of hope, it must have as its sole basis the certainty that God's fidelity to his own intrinsic nature (and that is precisely what is ultimately meant by the hallowing of his name) must necessarily lead to his sanctifying and renewing the people whom he has rejected.'

[15]In Ezk. 38:16, 23; 39:27 there are further promises that God will hallow his name among the nations by delivering his people from the mysterious forces of Gog. Note also the prayer of 2 Maccabees 1:25–26 for God to consecrate Israel to himself again, by purifying and preserving them from the oppression of the nations.

[16]Every divine commandment is thus 'an expression of the sanctifying act of God, of his sovereign arrangements for the separation of his people' (Berkouwer 1952: 24).

2. Sanctified in Christ

[1] *Cf.* Peterson 1992: 113–115. Jesus' challenge to traditional ways of thinking about cleansing suggests that a new way of sanctification may be in view.

[2] *Cf.* Dumbrell 1981: 1–21. Jesus moves from a re-identification of the true Israel in the Beatitudes (Mt. 5:2–12), to 'the corporate significance of the true Israel for both Jews and Gentiles' (5:13–16), to 'a restatement of the eschatological validity of the role of the law' 5:17–20).

[3] Without argument, I assume that the Fourth Gospel faithfully represents the teaching of Jesus, even though that teaching is presented in distinctively Johannine terms.

[4] Consecration for sacrifice is clearly implied in Jn. 17:19, according to Bultmann (1971: 510, note 5). *Cf.* Brown 1966: 766–767.

[5] *ek tou ponērou* in 17:15 could mean 'from evil' in the abstract sense, or 'from the evil one' in a personal sense. The latter is generally preferred by commentators because of the Johannine emphasis on the devil as the ruler of this world (12:31; 14:30; 16:11; *cf.* 1 Jn. 2:13–14; 3:12; 5:18–19).

[6] Porter (1992: 22) points out that the aorist is 'the least heavily weighted of the Greek verbal aspects, and hence carries the least significant meaning attached to the use of the form. In Greek the aorist is what some have called the "default" tense; that is, it is the tense chosen when there is no reason to choose another.'

[7] Such an interpretation is offered, for example, by Agnew (1974: 64–65), based on a misreading of the perfect periphrastic construction in Jn. 17:19.

[8] *Cf.* Brown 1966: 761. Brown thinks that both dimensions are to be understood in 17:17 but that the sense in 17:19 is that truth is rather 'the realm of the disciples' consecration than the agency of that consecration' (762).

[9] According to John 15:3, the disciples of Jesus had already been made 'clean' (Gk. *katharoi*) by the word he had spoken to them, 'pruned' by his teaching to bear fruit for God. Previously, in the footwashing incident, he had indicated to them that they could be 'clean' from sin because of his approaching sacrifice. In both contexts, Jesus speaks proleptically, anticipating his death, his return to the Father and the giving of the Holy Spirit. That great sequence of events brings the work of Jesus to fruition and fulfils his promise of cleansing from sin (13:10) and cleansing for service (15:3). So the prayer of John 17:17 ('sanctify them in the truth') is really a request for God to sustain them in the relationship which the Son makes possible *by his ministry as a totality.*

[10] *Cf.* Brown 1966: 766.

[11] In this chapter I will only consider the use of the verb *hagiazein*, which occurs in Heb. 2:11; 9:13; 10:10, 14, 29; 13:12. The use of the noun *hagiotēs* in 12:10 and the noun *hagiasmos* in 12:14 will be examined in chapter 4.

[12] The Hebrew original of Ps. 40:6 is 'ears you have dug for me' (NRSV, 'you have given me an open ear'). The best Greek manuscripts have the words found in Heb. 10:5 (*cf.* Ps. 39:7 LXX). The Hebrew is probably using the notion of a receptive ear to represent a life dedicated to serving God.

The Gk. expresses the underlying idea more clearly by means of the expression 'a body you have prepared for me'.

[13]Given the use of *ephapax* ('once for all') in 7:27; 9:12 (*cf. hapax* in 9:26–28), it is more likely that this adverb refers to the offering of the body of Jesus in 10:10 than to the expression *hēgiasmenoi esmen* ('we have been sanctified'). I discuss the link between Jesus' lifetime of obedience and his sacrificial death in *Hebrews and Perfection: An Examination of the Concept of Perfection in the 'Epistle to the Hebrews'* (see Peterson 1982: 148).

[14]The Gk. aorist passive participle *hēgēsamenos* is used in a summary way, to indicate how the readers came to share in the benefits of Christ's sacrifice.

[15]Westcott (1914: 317) wrongly takes the present participle in Heb. 10:14 to refer to 'all who from time to time realise progressively in fact that which has been potentially obtained for them'. Commenting on 2:11, he implies that a moral development is involved in this by relating it to 12:10. *Cf.* my discussion of Heb. 12:10, 14, in chapter 4.

[16]*Cf.* Peterson 1982: 126–127 for a detailed explanation of the perfecting of believers in Hebrews.

[17]The opposite of 'dead works' is the 'good works' (Heb. 10:24), which we are encouraged as God's people to pursue.

[18]*Cf.* Baumgärtel 1966: 606–607. The Gk. words for 'conscience' (*syneidos* and *syneidēsis*) only appear to have come into common use in the first century BC, though the verbal expression *synoida hemautō* had long been used to describe the process of self-reflection and self-awareness in both a moral and a non-moral sense (*cf.* Maurer 1971: 900–907). Both Paul and Hebrews seem to have been influenced by Jewish thinking about 'the heart' in their application of the language of conscience (*cf.* Maurer 1971: 907–919).

[19]*Cf.* Peterson 1992: 241–246.

[20]Fee (1987: 31–32) notes that the designation 'church' (Gk. *ekklēsia*) was used in the LXX to refer to Israel as the gathered people or 'congregation' of God. Paul similarly applies it to the gathered community of believers in Corinth (*cf.* 5:1–5; 11:18; 14:23). But the word is not simply used to emphasize the notion of gathering: 'It also came to serve as the primary designation for (Christians) as the newly constituted, eschatological people of God, who had submitted to the risen Christ as Lord, and thus awaited his return.'

[21]Ridderbos (1975: 261) speaks of this sanctification in terms of being 'appropriated and dedicated to God'. The church is then to live out or express that moral holiness that corresponds with its calling and election.

[22]Evans (1975: 196–200) argues that it is this eschatological concept of the saints as 'the true Israel, the Elect People of God, consecrated to serve his righteous cause in battle against his enemies, and destined to share in the glories of his coming kingdom, that provides the background to the New Testament use of *hoi hagioi* as a designation for Christians' (197).

[23]*Cf.* Robinson 1963: 45–53. Evans (1975: 197–198) is unnecessarily dismissive of such explanations of Paul's use of the terminology.

[24]A recent example of this is the intention of Roman Catholics to make Mary MacKillop Australia's 'first saint'. But there have been hundreds of

thousands of genuine saints in this country since the gospel first reached our shores. Their sainthood is ignored and diminished by such proposals!

[25] *Cf.* Van Unnik 1984: 533–551. He shows that in the OT, 'to call on God' has the special connotation of a prayer for help and salvation. When Christians are identified as 'those who call on the name of the Lord Jesus' they are similarly designated as those living in distress and praying to their Saviour for deliverance.

[26] Fung (1980: 248–250) wrongly argues that *hagiasmos* denotes a process of sanctification here, even though he notes that the participle *hēgiasmenois* (1 Cor. 1:2) refers 'not to the Corinthians' holiness in character or conduct but to their having been set apart to be God's holy people'.

[27] *Cf.* Barrett 1971: 60–61. Recent scholarly discussion about Paul's use of the noun *dikaiosynē* and the verb *dikaioun* ('to justify') is critiqued by O'Brien (1992: 69–95).

[28] *Cf.* my appendix on 'The meaning of *hagiasmos* in the New Testament'. If *hagiasmos* is actually describing a process in 1 Cor. 1:30, it can only be the process to which the verb *hagiazein* refers, which is that of being consecrated to God through the saving work of Jesus (*cf.* 1:2; 6:11).

[29] *Cf.* Porter 1993: 399.

[30] Fee (1987) rightly argues that the verbs are chosen for contextual rather than dogmatic reasons.

[31] Fung (1980: 250–251) rightly argues that the aorists in this verse are best taken as denoting coincidental action. The order of the verbs may be due to the fact that Paul wishes to describe the sanctifying effect of their conversion 'first in negative and then in positive terms (*apelousasthe, hēgiasthēte*)', with the reference to justification being added as 'a necessary part of the full statement of the effects of God's favour' (following O. Pfleiderer). But Fee (1987: 246) argues that the order of the verbs is 'theologically irrelevant'.

[32] Barrett (1971: 141) points out that the use of the non-technical *apelousasthe*, instead of *ebaptisthēte* ('you were baptised'), implies that 'it is the inward meaning rather than the outward circumstances of the rite that is important to Paul'. Fee (1987: 246–247) is less certain about baptismal associations in 1 Cor. 6:11. Nevertheless, he still equates 'washing' with regeneration through the Spirit, which is inconsistent with his view that the metaphor refers to the removal of 'the "filth" of the vice catalogue' in 6:9–10, in which case it is another way of talking about forgiveness.

[33] *Cf.* Carson 1992: 13–95; Seifrid 1992a.

[34] Barrett (1971) argues that Paul is referring to 'the moral effects of conversion' *in us*, rooted in the work of Christ *outside of us* and *for us*, and 'sealed in baptism'.

[35] Fee (1994) rightly opposes the view that each verb in the sequence corresponds to the persons of the Trinity (washed = Christ; sanctified = Spirit; justified = God).

[36] Fee (1994) stresses that the three verbs in 1 Cor. 6:11 describe different consequences of the saving death of Jesus for us. 'But because they were all experientially appropriated at conversion, which is essentially the work of the Spirit, they were also saved in these various aspects "by the Spirit of our God".'

3. Sanctified by word and spirit

[1] *Cf.* Wesley (1988) and Lindström (1950).

[2] In Dieter *et al*, *Five Views on Sanctification*, Dieter (1987: 36–46) offers a helpful survey of development in the period after Wesley. McQuilkin (1987: 149–183) gives 'The Keswick Perspective', and Horton (1987: 103–135) 'The Pentecostal Perspective'.

[3] I assume the Pauline authorship of Ephesians for the sort of reasons put forward by Barth (1974: 3–50).

[4] The aorist participle *katharisas* ('cleanse'), linked to the aorist subjunctive *hagiasē* ('sanctify'), need not imply that purification either precedes or follows sanctification. The moment of purification is doubtless the same as that of sanctification. *Cf.* Barth 1974: 626. Barth points out that both verbs have a cultic meaning originally and are used interchangeably in many contexts (625).

[5] Barth (1974: 691–699) concludes a discussion of possible interpretations with the assessment that 'the washing of water' refers to 'the new life given in common to all members of the church through the death of Christ and the Spirit of God'. Contra Bruce 1984: 388–389. Calvin's commentary on this verse takes 'the washing with water' as a reference to baptism and 'the word' as the promise which explains the value and use of that sacramental sign.

[6] Barth (1974: 627) comments: 'This Bridegroom's love is characterized by the will and power to effect a total transformation. He attributes qualities to the bride which she does not possess of her own.'

[7] Hoekema (1989) cites the conclusion of Herman Bavinck that 'faith is the outstanding means of sanctification'.

[8] In Eph. 1:14, the Holy Spirit is said to be 'the pledge of our inheritance', and this inheritance is further defined in terms of 'redemption as God's own people'. Again, in Col. 1:12, Paul speaks of sharing 'in the inheritance of the saints in light', which closely resembles the language of Acts 20:32; 26:18.

[9] Although the Gk. expression *tou haimatos tou idiou* could be rendered 'with his own blood' (NIV), that would be a unique way of describing the death of Christ. It is better to read 'his own' as a reference to 'his own Son' (*cf.* Ro. 8:32, Gk. *tou idiou hiou*). Bruce (1988: 391, note 56) points out that *ho idios* is well attested in Gk. papyri, where it is used as a term of endearment to near relations.

[10] 'The church of God' (*Gk. ekklēsia tou theou*) is the better reading in Acts 20:28, even though 'the church of the Lord' (Gk. *ekklēsia tou kyriou*) is very well attested. The latter seems to have been a later modification of the text to get over the awkwardness of saying that God acquired the church 'with his own blood'.

[11] Christians are similarly described as God's own 'possession' in Eph. 1:14 and 1 Pet. 2:9.

[12] Johnson (1992: 364) rightly points out that the expression in Acts 20:32 could also mean 'the message that comes from him by gift / favor' or 'the message / word that is his gift / favor'. But he ignores the importance of 20:24 as an interpretive key in this context.

[13]For an exposition of the theme of edification in Paul's teaching, *cf.* Peterson 1992: 206–215.

[14]Although the verb *hierourgein* does not occur in the LXX, it is used by Josephus and Philo with reference to the offering of the firstfruits, spiritual burnt offerings and the sacrifice of investiture. By derivation it means 'to perform the work of a priest', but it is also used in Jewish and non-Jewish texts in the broadest sense 'to present or offer sacrifices', without specifying whether or not a priest is responsible for the action. *Cf.* Schrenk 1966: 251–252.

[15]Many commentators take the expression 'the offering of the Gentiles' (Gk. *hē prosphora tōn ethnōn*) to mean 'the offering which consists of the Gentiles', implying that Paul offers the Gentiles to God like a priest. However, it would be more in accord with his liturgical expressions elsewhere to take 'the offering of the Gentiles' as 'the offering *made* by the Gentiles' (Murphy-O'Connor 1963: 288). O'Brien (1993: 31) argues that the phrase refers to *both* the Gentiles *and* their material gifts to the Jerusalem church.

[16]The dative in Rom. 15:6 is more likely to be instrumental ('by the Holy Spirit') than locative ('in the Holy Spirit').

[17]*Cf.* Peterson 1992: 173–179, and 1993: 271–288.

[18]*Cf.* O'Brien 1993: 33–34.

[19]*Cf.* Davies 1990: 25–30. Garlington (1990: 205–224) argues that *hypakoē pisteōs* expresses two ideas at the same time: 'the obedience which consists in faith and the obedience which is the product of faith' (223–224). However, I find it difficult to see how the genitive could convey both senses together.

[20]I have modified the NRSV translation by adopting the variant reading 'from the beginning' (Gk. *ap' archēs*), which is a little more widely attested than 'as the firstfruits' (Gk. *aparchēn*). The time reference is also more likely to have been the original in this context, where Paul refers to election for salvation. The apostle normally uses *aparchē* with a qualifying genitive. *Cf.* Best 1972: 312–314; O'Brien 1977: 187–188.

[21]Echoing Denney 1892: 342. Of course, the cross and resurrection of Jesus must be regarded as central to this 'system of theology', being the content of the gospel preached to the Thessalonians.

[22]There is no need to read the genitive here as objective and to translate 'sanctification of spirit' meaning 'of the human spirit' (*cf.* 1 Thes. 5:23). Absence of the definite article is not a barrier to the application of *pneuma* to God's Spirit in Rom. 8:4, 13–14. The expression *en hagiasmō pneumatos* is found in 1 Pet. 1:2, where the context indicates that consecration by the Spirit is intended.

[23]Best (1972: 315) notes that there are different ways of understanding the expression *pistei alētheias*. But 'if the parallelism with the first phrase is to be maintained then we ought to take *truth* as that which creates faith and the latter in the sense "trust", *truth* then stands for the gospel (*cf.* v. 12) which awakens faith'.

[24]Frame (1912) quotes Calvin to good effect: 'We find in ourselves a satisfactory proof (of election) if he has sanctified us by his Spirit, if he has enlightened us in the faith of his gospel.'

[25]It is possible that the three prepositional phrases in 1 Pet. 1:2 modify all of 1:1 and refer both to Peter and his readers. However, it is more natural to read the phrases as part of the entire dative construction that identifies the readers. *Cf.* Hiebert 1984: 37–38.

[26]The genitive is subjective, as in 2 Thes. 2:13, rather than objective, which would make it a reference to 'the sanctification of (our) spirit'.

[27]1 Pet. 1:3 defines regeneration in terms of the 'living hope' which Jesus makes possible through his resurrection from the dead. But, according to 1:23–25, we can only enjoy this hope if the message about Jesus is received in faith.

[28]NIV and NRSV have 'Jesus Christ' modifying both 'obedience' and 'sprinkling'. But reading the genitive 'of Jesus Christ' as objective in the first case ('obedience to Jesus Christ') and subjective in the second case ('by / with his blood') is awkward and unlikely. *Cf.* Hiebert 1984: 39; Michaels 1988: 11.

[29]'Children of obedience' is literally the expression in 1:14. This is a Hebraism, meaning 'those whose nature and character it is to be obedient'. It suggests a profound change from a life previously characterized by self-indulgence and by ignorance of God's character and will.

[30]The notion that God should be 'sanctified' in the midst of his people is strong in certain OT contexts (*e.g.* Lv. 10:3; Nu. 20:12–13; Ezk. 20:41; 28:22, 25). *Cf.* pp. 22–23.

[31]A wish-prayer is a petition to God expressed in the third person and using the optative mood in Greek ('May God . . .'). It is a report of how Paul prays for his converts, expressed in an epistolary form. Consequently, the readers are also addressed ('May God bless you . . .').

[32]*Cf.* Fee (1994: 65–66) for a helpful analysis of the grammatical and syntactical issues involved in translating 1 Thes. 5:23.

[33]*Cf.* Wiles 1974: 64.

[34]The adjective *holoteleis* agrees with *hymas* ('you'), so that the expression means literally 'sanctify you quite complete' (NIV, 'sanctify you through and through'). The synonym *holoklēron* is used in the second petition of this verse.

[35]The apostle then asks the Thessalonians to 'seal their restored harmony with the rite of the kiss of peace (v. 26)' and insists that his letter be read to *all*, 'friend and antagonist alike, so that none might escape the challenge of Paul's message' (Wiles 1974: 66–67).

[36]A distinction between the bodily and spiritual aspects of human nature is easily made, but 'to make a comparable distinction between "spirit" and "soul" is forced' (Bruce 1983: 130). Bruce shows partial parallels to the language of 1 Thes. 5:23 but says they throw little light on its details. Best (1972: 243–244) discusses different interpretations of this verse but comes to the same conclusion as Bruce about its meaning.

[37]*Cf.* Jewett (1971: 179–183) for the argument that Paul was attacking inadequate views of sanctification that were being presented to the Thessalonians.

[38]Martin Luther (1483–1536) insisted that 'to progress is always to begin again' (see Forde 1988: 28).

4. Pursuing holiness

[1]*E.g.* Packer 1992: 19–21.

[2]In Ryle's experience, 'God's holiest saints' agree that 'they see more, and know more, and feel more, and do more, and repent more, and believe more, as they get on in spiritual life, and in proportion to the closeness of their walk with God'.

[3]Here again we see Ryle echoing the Puritans, for whom 'a faith that did not manifest itself actively in life, a faith by which God did not seize the heart with power, such a faith was no faith but deception and death' (Hawkes 1990: 253).

[4]We must be holy 'because our present comfort depends much upon it' (Ryle 1952: 43).

[5]*Cf.* Bertram 1968: 596–625.

[6]*Cf.* Ps. 94(93):12; Job 5:17; 2 Macc. 6:12–17 and other Jewish sources noted by Attridge (1989).

[7]In this context, with a reference to (lit.) 'our fleshly fathers' in the preceding clause, it is likely that the expression 'Father of spirits' refers to God as our spiritual father or 'Father of [our] spirits'. *Cf.* Attridge 1989: 362–363.

[8]The noun *hagiotēs* came into use only late in hellenistic Judaism (*e.g.* 2 Macc. 15:2; *Test. Levi* 3:4). It is a variant in some manuscripts of 2 Cor. 1:12. Otherwise, it is not found in the NT apart from Heb. 12:10, where it is a summary way of speaking about the life and character of God. *Cf.* Lane 1991: 425.

[9]*Cf.* Ps. 85:11; Is. 32: 17; Jas. 3:18; Heb. 7:3.

[10]'Make straight paths for your feet' is not to be understood ethically in this context. Its point of reference is the ultimate goal of faith, 'which can be reached only through the endurance of stringent tests of faith' (Lane 1991: 427).

[11]Lane (1991: 444–446) gives an excellent summary of the argument of Hebrews 12, demonstrating the centrality of the exhortation in 12:14. Lane is much indebted to the insights of Käsemann (1960: 307–312).

[12]*Cf.* Foerster 1964: 406–417.

[13]NIV ('Make every effort . . . to be holy; without holiness no-one will see the Lord') and NEB ('Aim at . . . a holy life') are inadequate. AV, RSV, NRSV are less prejudicial. *Cf.* my Appendix A 'The meaning of *hagiasmos* in the New Testament'.

[14]'Within the community of faith, there is to be no separation of peace and holiness. If "peace" binds the community together as the achievement of Christ, "holiness" is that quality which identifies the community as the possession of Christ' (Lane 1991: 450).

[15]It is significant that Heb. 12:15 alludes to Dt. 29:17, with its suggestion that the whole community of God's people can be 'poisoned' by the behaviour of certain individuals. Dt. 29:17 has in mind the person who thinks he can act as he pleases and that God will not judge him.

[16]The construction *eis to stērixai* (1 Thes. 3:13, 'in order to strengthen / establish') suggests that the purpose of Paul's prayer in 3:12 is that their

hearts might be 'established blameless in holiness'. This is obscured by NIV, NRSV.

[17] *Cf.* O'Brien 1982: 203–204.

[18] The expression in Phil. 3:6 should not be pressed to mean that Paul completely fulfilled the law or entirely avoided transgressions. ' "Blameless" appears to describe an exemplary way of life that is in conformity with the OT as interpreted along Pharisaic lines' (O'Brien 1991: 380).

[19] Although a good case can be made for saying that the 'holy ones' are angels, Paul could also be including believing men and women in this reference (*cf.* 1 Thes. 4:14; 2 Thes. 1:10; Rom. 8:19). *Cf.* Bruce 1983: 73–74.

[20] *Cf.* Eph. 4:1 ('lead a life worthy of the calling to which you have been called'); Phil. 1:27 ('live your life in a manner worthy of the gospel of Christ'); Col. 1:10 ('lead lives worthy of the Lord').

[21] *Cf.* 2 Thes. 3:6–10; Col. 2:6–7 and my comment on Rom. 6:17 on page 102. Bruce (1983: 79) suggests that the ethical teaching was delivered 'in the form of a catechesis, grouped under such captions as "Put off (old vices)," "put on (new virtues)," "be subject (to those in authority and one to another)", "watch and pray" (*cf.* Col. 3:5 – 4:6).'

[22] 'To control your own body' (NRSV, NIV) is a more appropriate rendering of the Gk. *to heautou skeuos ktasthai* in this context than 'to take a wife for himself' (NRSV margin) or 'to live with his own wife' (NIV margin). *Cf.* Bruce 1983: 83. Contra Best 1972: 161–163.

[23] The change of preposition is significant. We are not called 'to / for impurity' (*epi akatharsia*) but 'in sanctification' (*en hagiasmō*). The last expression is also found in 2 Thes. 2:14 and 1 Pet. 1:2. There it is linked with the Spirit's work of consecrating people to God through faith in Christ.

[24] A related noun *hagiōsynē* is used in 1 Thes. 3:13, with reference to a quality of life, and it is likely that Paul used *hagiasmos* as a synonym in 4:3, 4, 7. *Cf.* Appendix A 'The meaning of *hagiasmos* in the New Testament'.

[25] Bruce (1983) discusses the sexual mores of the Greek world more fully on pp. 86–87.

[26] *Cf.* Reisser 1975: 487–501. The word-group can describe various modes of extra-marital sex 'insofar as they deviate from accepted social and religious norms (*e.g.* homosexuality, promiscuity, paedophilia, and especially prostitution)' (497).

[27] *Cf.* note 22 for alternative renderings of the Gk. expression *to heautou skeuos ktasthai* in 1 Thes. 4:4. Deidun (1981:19) observes that Paul's placing of these Gentile Christians in antithesis to 'Gentiles who do not know God' is a way of acknowledging them as God's true people under the New Covenant.

[28] The reasons for such an approach are well presented, and then dismissed, by Best (1972: 165–166). He rightly points out that this verse could be referring specifically to homosexual exploitation of a fellow Christian.

[29] This theme is developed in 1 Thes. 4:9–10, where the close link between holiness and love noted in other contexts is found again. In 4:11–12, Paul goes on to explore something of the 'commercial' implications of his teaching on Christian love.

[30] The position of *to hagion* ('holy') in the expression *to pneuma autou to*

hagion ('his holy Spirit') is emphatic, indicating that the Spirit is given to promote holiness in the lives of God's people. *Cf.* Rom. 1:4 (*pneuma hagiōsynēs*).

[31]Deidun (1981: 21) observes how this is consistent with OT teaching, in which 'God's presence is sanctifying and *therefore* demands holiness'. 'The dynamic that makes Paul's argument against sexual impurity possible is the experienced reality of the Spirit' (Fee 1994: 53).

[32]*Cf.* Deidun 1981: 20–21. This is another way of speaking about God's law being written in the heart (Je. 31:33). The Thessalonians' love for one another is 'the effect of God's immediate and efficacious action at the very source of their moral personality' (1981: 58).

[33]In the holy People of the New Covenant, 'the consecrating and unifying power of God's presence is interiorised' (Deidun 1981: 60).

[34]*Cf.* Furnish (1984: 367–383) for a helpful survey of alternative approaches. Against Furnish, there is some support in the immediate context for the view that Paul is warning against involvement in pagan idolatries (2 Cor. 6:15–16). *Cf.* Barrett 1973: 193–199.

[35]Beale (1989) shows how repeated temple and idolatry motifs arise naturally in conjunction with the theme of eschatological restoration in the OT texts cited by Paul. The Corinthians are urged not to evaluate Paul's apostleship according to the unbelieving standards of the world.

[36]*Cf.* Fee 1977: 140–161. Some of the Corinthians may have continued to reject his authority in this matter and the true implications of his gospel of grace. Hence the link with 6:1–13.

[37]*Cf.* Barrett 1971: 164–165; Fee 1987: 300–301. Fee suggests that this is analogous to Rom. 11:16, where the whole of Israel is 'holy' to the Lord, but not yet converted.

[38]Du Plessis (1959: 132) notes that 'sanctity calls for constant sanctification, by steadfast devotion and acts of self-sacrifice'. *Cf.* Delling 1972: 61–62 (the holiness given to the saints is something they 'actualize' by cleansing themselves from all that defiles both body and spirit).

[39]'Body and spirit' is another way of speaking about 'the whole person' here (*cf.* 1 Thes. 5:23). 'Since in Pauline understanding, idolatry in particular is the worship of demons (1 Cor. 10:20–22), it should not surprise us that here he concerns himself with cleansing from the "pollution of spirit". Not only must the "flesh" be gone, but also the "spirit" must be the place of the Spirit's habitation (1 Cor. 6:17), not a place where one is open to "spirits" ' (Fee 1994: 338).

[40]There are significant arguments for a late dating of the Pastorals and therefore for non-Pauline authorship. But I agree with Knight (1992: 4–52) that the case for Pauline authorship is stronger than any proposed alternative.

[41]The Gk. noun *eusebeia* is used in 1 Tim. 2:2; 3:16; 4:7–8; 6:3, 5–6, 11; 2 Tim. 3:5; Tit. 1:1, the verb *eusebein* in 1 Tim. 5:4, and the adverb *eusebōs* in 2 Tim. 3:12; Tit. 2:12. *Cf.* Acts 3:12; 10:2, 7; 17:23; 2 Pet. 1:3, 6, 7; 2:9; 3:11. An even more explicit term for 'godly devotion' (*theosebeia*) is used in 1 Tim. 2:10. Note also the references to 'ungodliness' (*asebeia* and its cognates) in Rom. 1:18; 4:5; 5:6; 11:26; 1 Tim. 1:9; 2 Tim. 2:16; Tit. 2:12; 1 Pet. 4:18; 2 Pet. 2:5–6; 3:7; Jude 4, 15, 18.

[42]Foerster (1971: 175–178) argues that in the Hellenistic–Roman period, when *eusebeia* mostly stood for the worship of the gods, 'the broader sense of respect for the orders of life still remains' (177). This is because the orders of life were seen to be under the protection of the gods.

[43]Wainwright (1993) particularly opposes the views of Dibelius & Conzelmann (1972: 39–41).

[44]*Cf.* Towner 1989: 147–154. Godliness unquestionably rests upon a soteriological foundation in the Pastorals.

5. Living between the cross and the resurrection

[1]A discussion of the relationship between justification and sanctification in Calvin's thought is found in McGrath 1986: 36–39.

[2]*Cf. Inst.* 3.2.33–37.

[3]*Cf.* Wallace 1959: 14–15. 'Everything that has been given to Christ in his sanctification is given for the very purpose of being communicated and imparted to the Church by the Spirit' (16).

[4]But 'a man cannot apply himself seriously to repentance without knowing himself to belong to God' (*Inst.* 3.3.2). *Cf.* Toon 1983: 75–80.

[5]Regeneration, however, is linked with Christian initiation in Scripture, and is not simply synonymous with the ongoing process of renewal in our lives. It should also be noted that Paul does not normally use the language of repentance in passages urging Christians to work out the implications of their new life in Christ.

[6]Against the traditional Protestant argument that 'the righteousness of God' refers to the righteousness from God which has been conferred upon us, Williams (1980: 241–290) argues that this term in the OT describes God as he is known in covenant relationship with Israel. A leading connotation of *dikaiosynē theou* in Romans is 'God's faithfulness in keeping his promise to Abraham' (265). This understanding enables Williams to set Paul's teaching about justification by faith within the framework of a wider covenant theology and still talk about the imputation of righteousness.

[7]'This judicial verdict, for which one had to wait according to Jewish theology until the last judgment, is according to Paul rendered the moment a person believes – hence the present tense of *dikaioumenoi*' (Moo 1991: 228).

[8]Against the view that 'works of the law' are simply Jewish 'identity markers' like circumcision, food laws, and Sabbath observance, *cf.* the excursus 'No One Will be Justified by Works of the Law' in Moo 1991: 212–218, and see Schreiner 1993: 41–71.

[9]*Cf.* Dunn (1988a: 242–244) for an assessment of various theories about the place of Romans 5 in the argument of the letter.

[10]Each of these three chapters begins with a clear-cut, unequivocal statement about the new situation of those who are in Christ (6:1–11, with reference to sin; 7:1–6, with reference to law; 8:1–9, with reference to flesh / mortal body). Paul then proceeds to qualify his statement in each

case by emphasizing the 'not-yet' dimension to our salvation (6:12–23; 7:7–25; 8:10–30).

[11]I am much indebted to Cranfield's insights regarding the four different senses in which we have died to sin, though I have differed from him in certain details. *Cf.* Moo 1991: 389–394, 426–433.

[12]In Col. 3:9, Paul uses the same Greek expression (*ho palaios hēmōn anthrōpos*) with reference to the action of believers, who have 'stripped off the old self with its practices'. This indicates that 'the Christian has still to fulfil on the moral level, by daily dying to sin, the death which in God's merciful decision and in the sacrament of baptism he has already died' (Cranfield 1975: 309). *Cf.* Moo (1991: 390–392) for a helpful critique of the 'two-natures' interpretation of Rom. 6:6.

[13]NEB translates *ho palaios hēmōn anthrōpos* 'the man we once were'.

[14]The aorist in Rom. 6:2 (Gk. *apethanomen*, 'we died') should not be taken to mean that Paul works with an ethic of sinlessness. The tense is 'exhortatively emphatic, to remind his readers that something decisive has happened to them' (Dunn 1988a: 307).

[15]*Cf.* Dunn (1988a: 327–330) for a discussion of what is actually meant by baptism in this context and what it achieves.

[16]Cranfield (1975: 307–308) takes the last clause of 6:5 to be a moral reference ('conformed [in our moral life] to his resurrection'). But this seems an unnatural reading of the future tense (Gk. *esometha*, 'we shall be') and of the verse as a whole. *Cf.* Dunn 1988a: 318. Cranfield uses the heading 'eschatological' for the fourth sense in which Christians die to sin, but this seems unsuitable. Given the fact that Paul is expounding an inaugurated eschatology, I prefer 'literal' as a description of the final stage.

[17]The verb *katargēthē* can range in meaning from 'render ineffective' to 'destroy'. Here, the implication of the aorist is not a final judgment already executed, but a decisive step taken to 'render powerless' (NIV) 'the body of sin'.

[18]The infinitive construction (*tou mēketi douleuein*) could be taken as a result, rather than as a purpose clause. More significantly, the present tense with 'no longer' warns believers of the real possibility of continuing in sin.

[19]*Cf.* Dunn 1988a: 320–321; Moo 1991:394–395. Use of the preposition *apo* ('from') after the verb *dedikaiōtai* suggests this meaning, rather than 'justified from'.

[20]Following Cranfield 1975: 315. Compare the use of the same verb in Rom. 3:28; 8:18; 14:14.

[21]'Mortal bodies' here in Rom. 6:12 is a reference to 'the whole man in his fallenness' (see 6:6). The present imperative *mē basileutō* ('do not let . . . reign') does not suggest that sin's reign may be terminated once and for all. It rather implies the need for ongoing resistance to sin. This verse thus anticipates the teaching of Romans 7:14–25.

[22]*Cf.* Furnish 1968: 195–196.

[23]*Cf.* Moo (1991: 404–408) for a helpful discussion of the phrase 'not under law but under grace'.

[24]The NRSV translation of 6:19, 'to greater and greater lawlessness', is unnecessary (so also NIV 'to ever-increasing wickedness'). It doubtless

arises from an understanding of the parallel *eis hagiasmon* in terms of progressive growth in holiness.

[25] *Cf.* Cranfield 1975: 327, 329. Dunn (1988a: 346–349) argues that the notion of 'consecration' or 'a dedicated state' is much more consistent with the biblical evidence, 'though a firm line between end result and process into cannot be clearly drawn'. *Cf.* my Appendix A 'The meaning of *hagiasmos* in the New Testament'.

[26] Furnish (1968: 153–157) provides a helpful discussion of the relationship between justification and sanctification in Paul's writings. 'Far from being the "ethical" counterpart to the "theological" doctrine of justification, the doctrine of sanctification in and of itself displays the unity of indicative and imperative' (156).

[27] Literally, Paul says 'you were put to death with respect to the law' (7:4, Gk. *ethanatōthēte tō nomō*). The 'body of Christ' here must mean 'the crucified body', not the church. Nevertheless, the death of Christ here, as in Rom. 6, is a corporate event in which believers share.

[28] *Cf.* Appendix B 'Sanctification and God's law'.

[29] From the meaning of 'human' in a neutral sense, *sarx* ('flesh') comes to mean 'that which is *solely* human, in distinction from, and in opposition to God' (Moo 1991: 442). *Cf.* Moo's Excursus, ' "Flesh" in Paul' (1991: 498–499), and Dunn 1988a: 363–364.

[30] Wright (1991: 197) argues that 'Paul's theological, not psychological, autobiography is included in this picture'. For a survey of alternative views, *cf.* Cranfield 1975: 342–344; Dunn 1988a: 381–383; Moo 1991: 448–456.

[31] To call the law 'spiritual' breaks down the sharp contrast of Rom. 7:6, suggesting that 'the law is not merely sin's cat's-paw, but nor am "I" yet free from sin'. Fee (1994: 510) argues that the law is 'spiritual' because it 'belongs to the Scriptures, which are God-breathed and therefore come by way of the Spirit'.

[32] *E.g.* Moo 1991: 469–478; Fee 1994: 509–515. But Dunn (1988a: 394) rightly questions the logic of the view that 'the passage here expresses with Christian hindsight the existential anguish of the pious Jew – which as a pious Jew he did not actually experience and which as a Christian he still does not experience!'

[33] *E.g.* Bruce 1963: 153; Mitton 1953–54: 78ff., 99ff., 132ff.

[34] Those who argue for mature believers to be included in Paul's reference here include Cranfield (1975: 344–347), Dunn (1988a: 404–406) and Packer (1984: 263–270). A helpful survey of opinions is provided by Seifrid (1992b: 313–333).

[35] Against Morrison & Woodhouse (1988: 9), it is not adequate to say that the person in Rom. 7:14–25 is 'man as he is in his "flesh" ', whether Christian or non-Christian.

[36] Cranfield (1975: 363) argues that this renewal is the work of God's Spirit.

[37] Dunn (1988a: 395) against Cranfield (1975: 364–365). *Cf.* Wright 1991: 208–214. But Fee (1994: 512, note 118) takes issue with the approach of Dunn and Wright.

[38] 'The split in the believing "I" matches the "split" in the law. The

willing "I" agrees with the law and thus bears witness that it is good. "I" accept the law's definition of God's will, and desire to do it, but still "I" fail' (Dunn 1988a: 407).

[39]So the deliverance from the law's captivity mentioned in Rom. 7:6 is qualified in 7:23 because we are caught up in the overlap between the ages, suspended between Christ's death and resurrection.

[40]'This body of death' (Gk. *tou sōmatos tou thanatos toutou*) refers to the body as occupied by sin and bound for death.

[41]As in other contexts, the word 'now' refers to the new era of salvation history inaugurated by Jesus' death and resurrection (*e.g.* Rom. 3:21; 5:9, 11; 6:22; 7:6). Morrison and Woodhouse (1988: 12–13) suggest a more direct link between 8:1 and the 'so then' of 7:25b (Gk. *ara oun*). But the flow of the argument they suggest demands an adversative in 8:1, rather than the resumptive 'therefore now' (Gk. *ara nyn*).

[42]But Moo follows Cranfield in taking *nomos* metaphorically here, to mean 'binding authority'.

[43]Dunn (1988a: 416–417) takes 'the law of the Spirit of life in Christ Jesus' to be the law 'rightly understood and responded to in the Spirit'. But this interpretation does not highlight sufficiently the Christological implications of this text. The same could be said of his interpretation of the purpose clause in Rom. 8:4.

[44]Wright (1991: 209–211) argues that *to dikaiōma tou nomou* means 'the decree that gives life in accordance with the commandment', so that, 'when God by his Spirit works to bring life to a person (Rom. 8:9–11), the desire and purpose of the Torah is thereby being fulfilled'. But this attempt to remove any sense of the law's *demand* loses touch with Paul's previous argument (*e.g.* 2:15, Gk. *to ergon tou nomou*, 'the work of the law'; 2:26, Gk. *ta dikaiōmata tou nomou*, 'the requirements of the law'). Cranfield (1975: 384) argues that the law's basic demand was faith expressed in obedience. Schreiner (1993: 152–154).

[45]*Cf.* Fee 1994: 534–538. Schreiner (1993: 150–152) rightly critiques those who understand Rom. 8:4 to be speaking solely of the objective fulfilment by Christ of the law's requirements. 'The work of Jesus on the cross is the basis and ground for believers fulfilling the law' (151).

[46]In Rom. 8:5–8 Paul is not describing 'the inner life of the believer' but '*two different* groups of people' (Fee 1994: 540). But the struggle of individual believers with the flesh is a manifestation of the fact that those who have the Spirit must live in a world where sin, death and the flesh are ruling powers.

[47]'Deeds of the body' will be a variant of 'living according to the flesh' (8:12). The idea of putting to death the deeds of the body 'by the Spirit' does not mean that the Spirit is a tool in the hands of Christians. A safeguard against such an interpretation is provided by the expression 'led by the Spirit' in 8:14. *Cf.* Cranfield 1975: 394–396.

[48]Calvin speaks of a 'twofold mortification of the flesh, 'one aspect of which relates to "those things which are around us" the other aspect of which is inward – the mortification of the understanding and the will' (Wallace 1959: 52). Note the exposition of Calvin's doctrine of mortification by Wallace (51–77, 94–100) and his treatment of vivification (78–93).

[49] *Cf.* Wallace 1959: 83. As long as we live in the flesh, our participation in the resurrection of Christ is severely limited.

6. Transformation, renewal and growth

[1] Note Furnish's critique of Beardslee's attempt to document progress and growth models in Paul (Furnish 1968: 240–241).

[2] Only in a very qualified sense, then, could sanctification be described as 'the earthly road which leads to the heavenly glory' (Cranfield 1975: 433).

[3] Although it is important to assert that women are included in this reference as well as men, the translation 'children of God' (Rom. 8:14 NRSV) obscures the fact that it is our relation to Jesus as *Son* of God (1:4, Gk. *huios tou theou*) that makes possible our 'adoption' (8:15, Gk. *huiothesia*) as 'sons of God' (8:14, Gk. *huioi tou theou*). The more general term 'children of God' is used in 8:16 (*tekna theou*).

[4] The fundamental work of the Spirit is to enable us to believe in the redemptive love of God, as that love was demonstrated in the saving work of Jesus (Rom. 5:5–8). Prayer to God as Father is a means by which the Spirit testifies to the adoption implicit in our justification by faith. *Cf.* Peterson 1990: 93–95.

[5] *Cf.* Foerster 1966: 776–781; Byrne 1979: 68–102.

[6] The expression 'heirs of God' (Gk. *klēronomoi theou*) may simply mean that God is the source of all that we inherit. In the context, it could also mean that we actually inherit the life and glory of God himself (*cf.* Cranfield 1975: 407).

[7] The Gk. conjunction *eiper* in Rom. 8:17 means 'if indeed, if after all', with reference to a further condition (*cf.* 8:9; Blass & Debrunner 1961: § 454). Its use here stresses the fact that a share in Christ's suffering and death is indispensable for sharing in the glory of his resurrection.

[8] Suffering with Christ (Rom. 8:17) includes the ideas of ' "for his sake", "in conformity with the pattern of his earthly life" (though not implying that our sufferings are redemptive in the sense in which his are), and "in union with him" (*i.e.* being bound to him by God's merciful decision so that we share his destiny)' (Cranfield 1975: 408).

[9] Redeemed creation fulfils the role for which it was intended when it is subjected to Christ as the last Adam (1 Cor. 15:27; Phil. 3:21), together with his 'many brothers' (Rom. 8:29). *Cf.* Dunn 1988a: 471.

[10] If the sequence in Romans 5:3–4 implies a process of maturing, it does not distinguish different stages of faith in Christians, 'since its end point is no different from the hope into which they entered on first believing (v. 2)' (Dunn 1988a: 250–251).

[11] Von Rad (1964: 238) argues somewhat artificially from the etymology of the Heb. word *kābôd* that the glory of the Lord is 'that which makes God impressive to man, the force of his self-manifestation'. If, in some contexts, this is associated with phenomena such as clouds and lightnings and fire, it is not to be thought that God is somehow identified with these things. They only serve to conceal the true power, majesty and magnificence of God,

which would destroy anyone to whom he might reveal himself fully (*cf.* Ex. 24:17; 33:20–23).

[12]*Cf.* Kittel 1964: 246–247; 1QH 17:15; CD 3:20.

[13]This 'knowledge' (Gk. *proegnō*) is to be understood in the Hebraic sense of experiencing and acknowledging a relationship (*cf.* Gn. 18:19; Je. 1:5; Am. 3:2). It does not mean that he looked into the future to see who would believe!

[14]Dunn (1988a: 483) argues that 'it is the sureness of the end as determined from the beginning which Paul wishes to emphasize'. So also Moo 1991: 571–572. Cranfield (1988a: 432) thinks that Rom. 8:29 is speaking about sanctification in terms of 'progressive conformity to Christ' and about glorification as the end of the process.

[15]In Pauline theology, 'life in the "already" means identification with Christ in his sufferings, so that in the "not yet" we shall also identify with him in his present glorification' (Fee 1994: 572).

[16]Dumbrell (1986: 179–194) argues that 'Paul sees the old covenant as not having been *abolished* but as having been *subsumed* or built upon, and that the essence of the Sinai covenant had been retained, as Jeremiah had argued that it would be (*cf.* Je. 31:31–34)' (187).

[17]*Cf.* Van Unnik 1973: 194–210.

[18]Wright (1991: 181) points out that Paul does not have to wear 'an even thicker veil, to hide the even greater glory' of the New Covenant, because his hearers do not need protecting from it as Moses' hearers did. Paul's ministry by the Spirit is appropriate for those who have the Spirit themselves and can look upon the glory 'with unveiled face'.

[19]*Cf.* Dunn 1970b: 309–320.

[20]Barrett (1973) argues that the translation 'reflecting as in a mirror' (Gk. *katoptrizomenoi*) removes 'the contrast of the Christians with the Jews, who because of their veil cannot see' (citing W. G. Kümmel). However, Fee (1994: 316–317) presents a strong case for the translation 'to behold as in a mirror'.

[21]The suggestion that Paul and the Corinthians are each 'an angled mirror, in which the other sees, reflected, the glory of the Lord' (Wright 1991: 185–189) is forced. The context is about turning to Christ himself and seeing the glory of God in him. Only in a secondary and derived sense do we see the glory reflected in one another.

[22]The same verb is used of the 'transfiguration' of Jesus in Mk. 9:2; Mt. 17:2. This is an anticipation and guarantee of the change promised to believers in the age to come.

[23]The adjective 'same' (Gk. *autēn*) suggests that the goal of transformation is the same for all believers, namely, becoming like Christ, who is the image of God (4:4, Gk. *eikōn tou theou*). *Cf.* Eph. 4:24.

[24]Paul maintains 'the characteristically biblical distance between God and man.'

[25]This is more likely than the view that 'from glory' indicates the source of the transformation and 'to glory' its result at the time of the resurrection.

[26]Harris (1983: 148) argues that 'one and the same Spirit initiates and completes the spiritual and somatic transformation of believers and then sustains their resurrection life'. *Cf.* Scott 1992: 256–266.

[27]Against those who view the corporate well-being of the congregation as the main focus of Paul's concern in Phil. 2:12-13, O'Brien (1991: 276-280) argues that it is 'an exhortation to common action, urging the Philippians to show forth the graces of Christ in their lives, to make their eternal salvation fruitful in the here and now as they fulfil their responsibilities to one another as well as to non-Christians' (280).

[28]The Gk. term *palingenesia* was much used by Stoicism to refer to the renewal of the world. When the term was adopted by Judaism it was given a biblical dimension and came to be used with reference to the new creation expected by the prophets (*cf.* Mt. 19:28, 'at the renewal of all things', Gk. *en tē palingenesia* = Lk. 22:30, 'in my kingdom'). *Cf.* Büchsel 1964: 686-689, 673-675.

[29]Dunn (1970a: 165-170) rightly points out that 'regeneration' (*palingenesia*) and 'renewal' (*anakainōsis*) are virtually synonymous and can hardly be taken to signify two quite distinct and separate events and experiences. To be reborn *is* to be made anew. *Cf.* Fee 1994: 781-783. My point, however, is that Paul's use of renewal terminology elsewhere suggests that the second part of the hendiadys in Titus 3:5 implies more than the first part.

[30]From a grammatical point of view, both 'the washing of regeneration' and 'renewal by the Holy Spirit' are dependent on the same preposition ('through', Gk. *dia*). 'The first pair of genitives focuses on the need for cleansing from past sin: "washing" and a word that speaks of that washing as an inner transformation, a "new beginning" ... The second pair focuses on the new life received and to be lived: The "Holy Spirit," the giver and sustainer of the new life, must do his work *within* Christians, and so is joined to a word that speaks of such a new life as an inner transformation, "renewal" ' (Knight 1992: 344).

[31]Dunn (1988b) endorses the distinction made by Harrisville: ' "conform" refers to a posture or attitude that may be changed at will, whereas "form" at the heart of "transformed" refers to what grows out of necessity from an inward condition'. Note the full discussion of these two verbs by Cranfield 1979: 605-608.

[32]Dunn (1988b: 714) notes that *dokimazein* normally has the sense of 'test, examine, approve', but that here it overlaps with the use of *diakrinein* (as used in 1 Cor. 14:29; *cf.* 1 Cor. 2:13-15; 12:10; *Did.* 11:7) to mean 'the capacity of forming the correct Christian ethical judgment at each given moment'. For Paul's teaching about the discernment of God's will, *cf.* Furnish 1968: 188-191, 227-237.

[33]The play on words in Gk. here suggests that, because people have rejected God as not worth reckoning with, he has delivered them into a condition 'in which their minds are fit only to be rejected as worthless, useless for their proper purpose, disreputable' (Cranfield 1975: 128).

[34]*Cf.* Thompson 1991: 82. It is also possible that Rom. 12:2 is meant to form a deliberate contrast with 2:18, where the Jews claim to know God's will and 'approve of what is superior' (Gk. *dokimazeis ta diapheronta*), because they are instructed in the law of God.

[35]*Cf.* Harris 1983: 129-130.

[36]When Paul talks about putting to death 'whatever in you is earthly'

(Col. 3:5), the expression in Gk. is literally 'the members which are upon earth' (*ta melē ta epi tēs gēs*). Here he seems to identify our 'members' with the sins they commit (*cf.* Rom. 6:13, 19; 7:23). They are called 'earthly', to continue the thought of Col. 3:2. The overall meaning is 'the sins which constitute the life of the earthly "old man" ' (3:9).

[37]Cf. O'Brien 1982: 188–189. The parallel passage in Eph. 4:22–24 supports the case for translating the participles as imperatives in Col. 3:9–10. However, the point that is being made with infinitives in Eph. 4:22–24 is somewhat different.

[38]The Gk. noun *hosiotēs* ('holiness') only occurs here in the NT. The adjective *hosios* in the LXX renders the Heb. *hāsîd* ('loyal', 'pious').

[39]Note M. Barth's extended note on the transfer from the Old Man to the New (Barth 1974: 536–545).

[40]See Barth 1974: 440–441. Barth argues that one goal is described by three parallel expressions beginning with *eis*. The verb *katantaō* implies movement towards an object (*cf.* 1 Cor. 14:36) and may suggest in this context a 'solemn meeting' with Christ at his second coming, when the church will be conformed to his glory (*cf.* Eph. 5:27; Phil. 3:20–21; Rom. 8:29–30; Col. 3:4). *Cf.* his Comment VII.

[41]This translation by M. Barth is justified by his detailed analysis of the key words in this text and their relationship to each other (1974: 447–450).

Appendix A

[1]Note the predominantly cultic application of *hagizein* and related terms, as listed by Liddell & Scott 1940: 9.

[2]Procksch, 1964: 113, citing Blass & Debrunner 1961: § 109.

[3]The cultic sense of consecration comes to the fore in many references to baptism and the Lord's Supper.

[4]The use of this noun 'in a moral sense for a process or, more often, its result (the state of being made holy) is peculiar to our lit.' (Bauer *et al* 1979: 9).

Appendix B

[1]Calvin's summary of the three uses of the law is found in *Inst.* 2.7.6–13.

[2]Cf. Berkouwer (1952: 163–193) for a more detailed historical and theological review of the Reformed position.

[3]Cf. Packer 1984: 112–114, 'The rule of holiness is God's revealed law'; VanGemeren 1993: 13–58.

[4]Forde (1988: 81) continues, 'Only Christ, grasped in faith, is the end of the law, not the Christian and certainly not Christian theology or ethics'.

[5]Note Fee's discussion of the way the 'fulfilled Torah' works out in the lives of those whom the life-giving Spirit has set free from 'the law of sin and death' (1994: 535–538, 556–564).

[6]Cf. Cranfield (1975: 319–320, 336, 338) and Hübner (1984: 134–135). We introduce categories that are foreign to Paul by distinguishing between

the law in its condemning power and the law as a 'rule of life' (*cf.* Moo 1991: 440).

[7]Dunn (1988a) describes the Jews as putting themselves so fully under the law as peculiarly theirs that 'they have treated the law in effect as a spiritual power appointed by God to be as it were their national guardian angel'.

[8]Moo (1991) reminds us that in Paul's view the Mosaic law had a definite sin-producing and sin-intensifying function (*cf.* Rom. 3:20; 4:15; 5:13–14, 20; 7:7–11, 13; 1 Cor. 15:56).

[9]*Cf.* Moo's comments on Rom. 7:4 (1991: 438–442), and his essay 'The Law of Christ as the Fulfillment of the Law of Moses' (1993: 319–376).

[10]Against Räisänen (1983: 46–47) and Westerholm (1988: 198–205), we may not conclude that the law can play no role at all in the life of the Christian.

[11]*Cf.* Schreiner 1993: 160–178.

[12]It is inadequate to conclude that, if love 'sums up' the commandments, 'the one who truly loves will have no need of these commandments' (Moo 1993: 359).

[13]A large measure of continuity existed between the New Covenant and the Mosaic law, but Paul did not believe that in the eschatological era the Mosaic covenant would be restored. *Cf.* Thielman's comments about sanctity and the law in the Corinthian letters (1994: 86–99).

[14]*Cf.* Furnish 1968: 227–237.

[15]In my discussion of Rom. 8:3–4 (110–111), I argue that God not only provides in Christ the full completion of the law's demands for us, but also sends the Spirit into our hearts to empower a new obedience to his demands.

[16]*Cf.* Wintle 1979: 42–50; Moo 1993: 367–370.

[17]I am not sure, however, that Moo (1993) gives adequate place to the need for continuing reflection on the law of Moses and application of its principles by Christians.

[18]*Cf.* Sanders (1983: 3–10), expanding and developing aspects of his earlier book (1977: 431–556).

[19]Note particularly Sanders' section 'The Law and the Consequences of Transgression and Obedience' (1983: 105–114), where he argues that, through disobedience, 'Christians can revert to the non-Christian state and share the fate of unbelievers' (111).

[20]Concretely, the law was modified 'by the revelation of the universal lordship of Christ and consequently by the requirements of the Gentile mission' (Sanders 1983: 114).

[21]*Cf.* Schreiner 1993: 93–121, 180–182.

[22]Note the assessment of contemporary attempts to relate justification by faith and judgment according to works by O'Brien (1992: 89–95).

Index of Scripture references

OLD TESTAMENT

Index of modern authors

Bibliography

Agnew, M. S. (1974), *Transformed Christians: New Testament Messages on Holy Living*, Kansas City, MO: Beacon Hill.

Alexander, D. L., ed. (1988), *Christian Spirituality: Five Views of Sanctification*, Downers Grove, IL: InterVarsity Press.

Attridge, H. W. (1989), *The Epistle to the Hebrews*, Hermeneia, Philadelphia: Fortress.

Barnett, P. W. (1988), *The Message of 2 Corinthians: Power in Weakness*, The Bible Speaks Today, Leicester / Downers Grove, IL: Inter-Varsity Press.

Barrett, C. K. (1971), *A Commentary on the First Epistle to the Corinthians*, Black's New Testament Commentary, 2nd ed., London: Black.

— (1973), *The Second Epistle to the Corinthians*, Black's New Testament Commentary, London: Black.

Barth, M. (1974), *Ephesians 4–6*, Anchor Bible 34A, New York: Doubleday.

Bauer, W. (1979), *A Greek–English Lexicon of the New Testament and Other Early Christian Literature* (trans. and ed. by W. F. Arndt & F. W. Gingrich, 1957; 2nd rev. ed. F. W. Gingrich & F. W. Danker, 1979), Chicago: University of Chicago Press; Cambridge: Cambridge University Press.

Baumgärtel, F. (1966), in *TDNT*, vol. 3, pp. 606–607.

Beale, G. K. (1989), 'The Old Testament Background of Reconciliation in 2 Corinthians 5–7 and its Bearing on the Literary Problem of 2 Corinthians 6.14 – 7.1', *New Testament Studies* 35, pp. 550–581.

Beare, F. W. (1958–59), 'On the Interpretation of Romans VI.17', *New Testament Studies* 5, pp. 206–210.

Behm, J. (1967), in *TDNT*, vol. 4, pp. 755–759.

Berkouwer, G. C. (1952), *Faith and Sanctification*, Grand Rapids: Eerdmans.

Bertram, G. (1968), in *TDNT*, vol. 5, pp. 596–625.

Best, E. (1972), *The First and Second Epistles to the Thessalonians,* Black's New Testament Commentary, London: Black.

Blass, F., & A. Debrunner (1961), *A Greek Grammar of the New Testament and Other Early Christian Literature* (R. W. Funk, ed.), Chicago: University of Chicago Press.

Bockmuehl, K. (1988), 'Sanctification', in *New Dictionary of Theology* (S. B. Ferguson & D. F. Wright, eds.), Leicester / Downers Grove, IL: Inter-Varsity Press.

Brown, R. E. (1966), *The Gospel According to John (xiii–xxi),* Anchor Bible 29A, New York: Doubleday 1966; London: Chapman 1971.

Bruce, F. F. (1963), *The Epistle to the Romans,* Tyndale New Testament Commentary, London: Tyndale Press.

— (1964), *The Epistle to the Hebrews,* London: Marshall, Morgan & Scott; Grand Rapids: Eerdmans.

— (1977), *Paul: Apostle of the Free Spirit,* Exeter: Paternoster.

— (1983), *1 & 2 Thessalonians,* Word Biblical Commentary, Waco, TX: Word.

— (1984), *The Epistles to the Colossians, to Philemon and to the Ephesians,* New International Commentary on the New Testament, Grand Rapids: Eerdmans.

— (1988), *The Book of the Acts,* New International Commentary on the New Testament, rev. ed., Grand Rapids: Eerdmans.

Büchsel, F. (1964), in *TDNT,* vol. 1, pp. 673–675.

Bultmann, R. (1971), *The Gospel of John: A Commentary,* ET, Oxford: Blackwell; Philadelphia: Westminster.

Byrne, B. (1979), *'Sons of God' – 'Seed of Abraham': A Study of the Idea of Sonship of God of All Christians in Paul against the Jewish Background,* Analecta Biblica 83, Rome: Biblical Institute.

Calvin, J. (*Heb–Pet*), *The Epistle of Paul the Apostle to the Hebrews and the First and Second Epistles of St Peter* (trans. W. B. Johnston, 1963), Edinburgh / London: Oliver & Boyd.

— (*Inst.*), *Institutes of the Christian Religion* (trans. F. L. Battles, 1961), London: SCM Press; Philadelphia: Westminster.

— (*Rom–Gal*), *Calvin's Commentaries, Vol. 11: Romans–Galatians,* Wilmington: Associated Publishers and Authors.

Carson, D. A. (1991), *The Gospel According to John,* Leicester: Inter-Varsity Press; Grand Rapids: Eerdmans.

— ed. (1992), *Right with God: Justification in the Bible and the World,* Exeter: Paternoster; Grand Rapids: Baker for World Evangelical Fellowship.

Cranfield, C. E. B (1975), *A Critical and Exegetical Commentary on the Epistle to the Romans*, vol. 1, International Critical Commentary, Edinburgh: T. & T. Clark.

— (1979), *The Epistle to the Romans*, vol. 2, International Critical Commentary, Edinburgh: T. & T. Clark.

Davies, G. N. (1990), *Faith and Obedience in Romans*, Journal for the Study of the New Testament Supplement 39, Sheffield: JSOT Press.

Deidun, T. J (1981), *New Covenant Morality in Paul*, Analecta Biblica 89, Rome: Biblical Institute.

Delling, G. (1972), in *TDNT*, vol. 8, pp. 61–62.

Denney, J. (1892), *The Epistles to the Thessalonians*, London: Hodder.

Dibelius, M., & H. Conzelmann (1972), *The Pastoral Epistles: A Commentary on the Pastoral Epistles*, Hermeneia, ET, Philadelphia: Fortress.

Dieter, M. E. (1987), 'The Wesleyan Perspective', in *Five Views on Sanctification* (M. E. Dieter *et al*), Grand Rapids: Academie.

Dieter, M. E., A. A. Hoekema, S. M. Horton, J. Robertson McQuilkin & S. F. Walvoord (1987), *Five Views on Sanctification*, Grand Rapids: Academie.

Douglas, M. (1966), *Purity and Danger*, London: Routledge & Kegan Paul.

Dumbrell, W. J. (1981), 'The Logic of the Role of the Law in Matthew V 1–20', *Novum Testamentum* 23, pp. 1–21.

— (1984), *Covenant and Creation: An Old Testament Theology*, Flemington Markets, Lancer; Exeter: Paternoster.

— (1986), 'Paul's use of Exodus 34 in 2 Corinthians 3', in *God who is Rich in Mercy: Essays presented to D. B. Knox* (P. T. O'Brien & D. G. Peterson, eds.), Sydney: Lancer; Grand Rapids: Baker.

Dunn, J. D. G. (1970a), *Baptism in the Holy Spirit*, London: SCM Press.

— (1970b), '2 Corinthians iii.17 – the Lord is the Spirit', *Journal of Theological Studies* 21, pp. 309–320.

— (1988a), *Romans 1–8*, Word Biblical Commentary 38A, Waco, TX: Word.

— (1988b), *Romans 9–16*, Word Biblical Commentary 38B, Waco, TX: Word.

Du Plessis, P. J. (1959), ΤΕΛΕΙΟΣ: *The Idea of Perfection in the New Testament*, Kampen: Kok.

Eichrodt, W. (1961), *Theology of the Old Testament*, vol. 1, ET,

London: SCM Press.

— (1970), *Ezekiel: A Commentary*, ET, London: SCM Press.

Evans, O. E. (1975), 'New Wine in Old Skins: XIII. The Saints', *Expository Times* 86, pp. 196–200.

Fee, G. D. (1977), 'II Corinthians VI.14 – VII.1 and Food Offered to Idols', *New Testament Studies* 23, pp. 140–161.

— (1987), *The First Epistle to the Corinthians*, New International Commentary on the New Testament, Grand Rapids: Eerdmans.

— (1994), *God's Empowering Presence: The Holy Spirit in the Letters of Paul*, Peabody, MA: Hendrickson.

Ferguson, S. B. (1988), 'The Reformed View', in *Christian Spirituality: Five Views of Sanctification* (D. L. Alexander, ed.), Downers Grove, IL: InterVarsity Press.

Fitzmyer, J. A. (1992), *Romans*, Anchor Bible 33, New York: Doubleday.

Foerster, W. (1964), in *TDNT*, vol. 2, pp. 406–417.

— (1966), in *TDNT*, vol. 3, pp. 776–781.

— (1971), in *TDNT*, vol. 7, pp. 175–178.

Forde, G. O. (1988), 'The Lutheran View', in *Christian Spirituality: Five Views of Sanctification* (D. L. Alexander, ed.), Downers Grove, IL: InterVarsity Press.

Frame, J. E. (1912), *A Critical and Exegetical Commentary on the Epistles of St Paul to the Thessalonians*, International Critical Commentary, Edinburgh: T. & T. Clark.

Fung, R. Y.-K (1980), 'Justification by Faith in 1 & 2 Corinthians', in *Pauline Studies: Essays presented to F. F. Bruce* (D. A. Hagner & M. J. Harris, eds.), pp. 248–250, Exeter: Paternoster; Grand Rapids: Eerdmans.

Furnish, V. P. (1968), *Theology and Ethics in Paul*, Nashville, TN: Abingdon.

— (1984), *II Corinthians*, Anchor Bible 32A, Garden City, NY: Doubleday.

Gammie, J. G. (1989), *Holiness in Israel*, Minneapolis, MN: Fortress.

Garlington, D. (1990), 'The Obedience of Faith in the Letter to the Romans. Part I: The meaning of *hypakeō pisteōs* (Rom. 1:5; 16:26)', *Westminster Theological Journal* 52, pp. 201–224.

Gundry, R. H. (1985), 'Grace, Works and Staying Saved in Paul', *Biblica* 60, pp. 1–38.

Harris, M. J. (1983), *Raised Immortal: The Relation Between*

Resurrection and Immortality in New Testament Teaching, London: Marshall, Morgan & Scott.

Hawkes, R. M. (1990), 'The Logic of Assurance in English Puritan Theology', *Westminster Theological Journal* 52, pp. 247–261.

Hiebert, D. E. (1984), *First Peter: An Expositional Commentary*, Chicago: Moody.

Hoekema, A. A. (1987), 'The Reformed Perspective', in *Five Views on Sanctification* (M. E. Dieter *et al*), Grand Rapids: Academie.

— (1989), *Saved by Grace*, Grand Rapids: Eerdmans; Exeter: Paternoster.

Horton, S. M. (1987), 'The Pentecostal Perspective', in *Five Views on Sanctification* (M. E. Dieter *et al*), Grand Rapids: Academie.

Hübner, H. (1984), *Law in Paul's Thought*, Edinburgh: T. & T. Clark.

Jacob, E. (1974), in *TDNT*, vol. 9, pp. 626–627.

Jewett, R. (1971), *Paul's Anthropological Terms: A Study of their Use in Conflict Settings*, Arbeiten zur Geschichte des Antiken Judentums und des UrChristentums, vol. 10, Leiden: Brill.

Johnson, L. T. (1992), *The Acts of the Apostles*, Sacra Pagina 5, Collegeville, MN: Michael Glazier / Liturgical Press.

Käsemann, E. (1960), 'Hebräer 12, 12–17', in *Exegetische Versuche und Besinnungen*, vol. 1, Göttingen: Vandenhoeck & Ruprecht.

— (1980), *Commentary on Romans*, ET, Grand Rapids: Eerdmans; London: SCM Press.

Kittel, G. (1964), in *TDNT*, vol. 2, pp. 246–247.

Knight III, G. W. (1992), *The Pastoral Epistles: A Commentary on the Greek Text*, New International Greek Testament Commentary, Grand Rapids: Eerdmans; Carlisle: Paternoster.

Lampe, G. W. H. (1961), *A Patristic Greek Lexicon*, Oxford: Clarendon.

Lane, W. L. (1991), *Hebrews 9–15*, Word Biblical Commentary 47B, Waco, TX: Word.

Leenhardt, F. J. (1961), *The Epistle to the Romans: A Commentary*, ET, London: Lutterworth.

Liddell, H. G., & R. Scott (1940), *A Greek–English Lexicon* (H. S. Jones & R. McKenzie, 9th rev. ed.), Oxford: Clarendon.

Lindström, H. (1950), *Wesley and Sanctification: A Study in the Doctrine of Salvation*, London: Epworth.

McGrath, A. E. (1986), *Iustitia Dei: A History of the Christian*

Doctrine of Justification, Vol. 2: From 1500 to the Present Day, Cambridge: Cambridge University Press.

— (1993), 'Justification', in *Dictionary of Paul and his Letters* (G. F. Hawthorne, R. P. Martin & D. G. Reid, eds.), Downers Grove, IL/Leicester: Inter-Varsity Press.

McQuilken, J. Robertson (1987), 'The Keswick Perspective', in *Five Views on Sanctification* (M. E. Dieter *et al*), Grand Rapids: Academie.

Maurer, C. (1971), in *TDNT*, vol. 7, pp. 899–919.

Michaels, J. R. (1988), *1 Peter*, Word Biblical Commentary 49, Waco, TX: Word.

Michel, O. (1975), *Der Brief an die Hebräer*, Meyers Kommentar, 13th ed., Göttingen: Vandenhoeck & Ruprecht.

Mitton, C. L. (1953–54), 'Romans vii Reconsidered', *Expository Times* 65, pp. 78–81, 99–103, 132–135.

Moo, D. J. (1991), *Romans 1–8*, The Wycliffe Exegetical Commentary, Chicago: Moody.

— (1993), 'The Law of Christ as the Fulfillment of the Law of Moses: A Modified Lutheran View', in G. L. Bahnsen, W. C. Kaiser, D. J. Moo, W. G. Strickland & W. A. VanGemeren, *The Law, the Gospel and the Modern Christian: Five Views*, pp. 319–376, Grand Rapids: Zondervan.

Morrison, B., & J. Woodhouse (1988), 'The Coherence of Romans 7:1 – 8:8', *Reformed Theological Review* 47, pp. 8–16.

Motyer, J. A. (1993), *The Prophecy of Isaiah*, Leicester: Inter-Varsity Press.

Moulton, J. H., & G. Milligan (1930), *The Vocabulary of the Greek Testament Illustrated from the Papyri and other Non-Literary Sources*, Grand Rapids: Eerdmans; London: Hodder & Stoughton.

Murphy-O'Connor, J. (1963), *Paul on Preaching*, London: Sheed & Ward.

Murray, J. (1977), *Collected Writings*, vol. 2, Carlisle, PA/Edinburgh: Banner of Truth.

O'Brien, P. T. (1977), *Introductory Thanksgivings in the Letters of Paul*, Supplement to *Novum Testamentum* 49, Leiden: Brill.

— (1982), *Colossians, Philemon*, Word Biblical Commentary 44, Waco, TX: Word.

— (1991), *The Epistle to the Philippians: A Commentary on the Greek Text*, New International Greek Testament Commentary, Grand Rapids: Eerdmans.

— (1992), 'Justification in Paul and Some Crucial Issues in the

Last Two Decades', in *Right with God: Justification in the Bible and the World* (D. A. Carson, ed.), pp. 69–75, Exeter: Paternoster; Grand Rapids: Baker for World Evangelical Fellowship.

— (1993), *Consumed by Passion: Paul and the Dynamic of the Gospel*, Homebush West: Lancer.

Packer, J. I. (1984), *Keep in Step with the Spirit*, Old Tappan, NJ: Revell; Leicester: Inter-Varsity Press.

— (1992), *Pursuing Holiness*, Cambridge: Crossway.

Peterson, D. G. (1982), *Hebrews and Perfection: An Examination of the Concept of Perfection in the 'Epistle to the Hebrews'*, Society for New Testament Studies Monograph Series 47, Cambridge: Cambridge University Press.

— (1990), 'Prayer in Paul's Writings', in *Teach us to Pray: Prayer in the Bible and the World* (D. A. Carson, ed.), Carlisle: Paternoster; Grand Rapids: Baker.

— (1992), *Engaging with God: A Biblical Theology of Worship*, Leicester: Apollos 1992; Grand Rapids: Eerdmans 1993.

— (1993), 'Worship and Ethics in Romans 12', *Tyndale Bulletin* 44.2, pp. 271–288.

Porter, S. E. (1992), *Idioms of the Greek New Testament*, Sheffield: JSOT Press.

— (1993), 'Holiness, Sanctification', in *Dictionary of Paul and his Letters* (G. F. Hawthorne, R. P. Martin & D. G. Reid, eds.), Downers Grove, IL / Leicester: Inter-Varsity Press.

Procksch, O. (1964), in *TDNT*, vol. 1, pp. 89–97, 113.

Räisänen, H. (1983), *Paul and the Law*, Philadelphia: Fortress.

Reisser, H. (1975), in *New International Dictionary of New Testament Theology* (C. Brown, ed.), vol. 1, pp. 497–501, Exeter: Paternoster.

Ridderbos, H. (1975), *Paul: An Outline of his Theology*, ET, Grand Rapids: Eerdmans.

Robinson, D. W. B. (1963), 'Who were "the saints"?', *Reformed Theological Review* 22, pp. 45–53.

Ryle, J. C. (1952), *Holiness: Its Nature, Hindrances, Difficulties and Roots*, London: James Clarke.

Sanders, E. P. (1977), *Paul and Palestinian Judaism: A Comparison of Patterns of Religion*, London: SCM Press.

— (1983), *Paul, the Law and the Jewish People*, Philadelphia: Fortress.

Schreiner, T. R. (1993), *The Law and its Fulfillment: A Pauline*

189

Theology of Law, Grand Rapids: Baker.

Schrenk, G. (1966), in *TDNT*, vol. 3, pp. 251–252.

Scott, J. M. (1992), *Adoption as Sons of God*, Wissenschaftliche Untersuchungen zum Neuen Testament 2:48, Tübingen: Mohr.

Seifrid, M. A. (1992a), *Justification by Faith: The Origin and Development of a Central Theme*, Brill: Leiden.

— (1992b), 'The Subject of Rom. 7:14–25', *Novum Testamentum* 34, pp. 313–333.

Snaith, N. H. (1944), *The Distinctive Ideas of the Old Testament*, London: Epworth.

Stott, J. R. W. (1966), *Men Made New: An Exposition of Romans 5–8*, London: Inter-Varsity Fellowship.

Thielman, F. (1994), *A Contextual Approach: Paul and the Law*, Downers Grove, IL: InterVarsity Press.

Thompson, M. (1991), *Clothed with Christ: The Example and Teaching of Jesus in Romans 12:1 – 15.13*, Journal for the Study of the New Testament Supplement 59, Sheffield: Sheffield Academic Press.

Toon, P. (1983), *Justification and Sanctification*, Foundation for Faith series, Westchester, IL: Crossway.

Towner, P. H. (1989), *The Goal of our Instruction*, Sheffield: JSOT Press.

Van Rensburg, S. P. J. J. (1967), 'Sanctification according to the New Testament', *Neotestamentica* 1, pp. 73–87.

Van Unnik, W. C. (1973), 'With Unveiled Face: An Exegesis of 2 Corinthians iii:12–18', in *Sparsa Collecta: The Collected Essays of W. C. van Unnik*, Leiden: Brill.

— (1984), 'With all those who call on the name of the Lord', in *The New Testament Age: Essays in Honor of Bo Reicke* (W. C. Weinrich, ed.), vol. 2, pp. 533–551, Macon: Mercer.

VanGemeren, W. A. (1993), 'The Law is the Perfection of Righteousness in Jesus Christ: A Reformed Perspective', in G. L. Bahnsen, W. C. Kaiser, D. J. Moo, W. G. Strickland & W. A. VanGemeren, *The Law, the Gospel and the Modern Christian: Five Views*, Grand Rapids: Zondervan.

Von Rad, G. (1964), in *TDNT*, vol. 2, p. 238.

Wainwright, J. J. (1993), '*Eusebia*: Syncretism or Conservative Contextualization?', *Evangelical Quarterly* 65.3, pp. 211–224.

Wallace, R. S. (1959), *Calvin's Doctrine of the Christian Life*, Edinburgh / London: Oliver & Boyd.

Wenham, G. J. (1979), *The Book of Leviticus*, New International Commentary on the Old Testament, Grand Rapids: Eerdmans.

Wesley, J. (1988), *A Plain Man's Guide to Holiness* (originally published as *A Plain Account of Christian Perfection*), (H. C. Backhouse, ed.), London: Hodder.

Westcott, B. F. (1914), *The Epistle to the Hebrews*, 3rd ed., London: Macmillan.

Westerholm, S. (1988), *Israel's Law and the Church's Faith: Paul and his Recent Interpreters*, Grand Rapids: Eerdmans.

Wiles, G. P. (1974), *Paul's Intercessory Prayers: The Significance of the Intercessory Prayer Passages in the Letters of St Paul*, Society for New Testament Studies Monograph Series 24, Cambridge: Cambridge University Press.

Williams, S. K. (1980), 'The "Righteousness of God" in Romans', *Journal of Biblical Literature* 99, pp. 241–290.

Wintle, B. (1979), 'Paul's Conception of the Law of Christ and its Relation to the Law of Moses', *Reformed Theological Review* 38, pp. 42–50.

Wood, L. W. (1988), 'A Wesleyan Response', in *Christian Spirituality: Five Views of Sanctification* (D. L. Alexander, ed.), Downers Grove, IL: InterVarsity Press.

Wright, D. P. (1992), 'Holiness (OT)', in *Anchor Bible Dictionary* (D. N. Freedman, ed.), vol. 3, pp. 239–248, Doubleday: New York.

Wright, N. T. (1991), *The Climax of the Covenant Christ and the Law in Pauline Theology*, Edinburgh: T. & T. Clark.